Guide to
Floating Whitewater Rivers

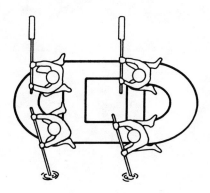

R. W. Miskimins

Photos: Bette & Kevin Miskimins
Drawings: Esther Poleo

ISBN 0-936608-49-8 • Copyright 1987 R. W. Miskimins
Typesetting: Chris Mazzuca • Book Design: Joyce Herbst
Printed in U.S.A.
Frank Amato Publications
P. O. Box 02112 • Portland, OR 97202 • (503) 653-8108

About the Author:

R. W. (Ray) Miskimins is a clinical psychologist, in private practice
and clinical director of a small inpatient psychiatric facility in Grants
Pass, Oregon. He was raised in Portland, Oregon, and while growing
up fished two or three dozen of that state's great rivers. About ten
years ago he moved to Grants Pass, home of the famous Rogue River,
and began his love affair with whitewater boating. For nearly a
decade he has spent uncounted hours and days at the oars or paddle,
of his drift boat, raft, cataraft, inflatable kayak, and canoe. With
over 50 articles and books to his credit during the past 20 years, it
only remained for him to share his experience in print.

Contents

Preface

A ROUND THE SUBJECT OF WHITEWATER RIVERS MY wife says I'm a "fanatic," and she's probably right. Everyone should have a few passions and two great ones are river running and steelhead fishing—if I get the chance, I'll do both at the same time.

Many people have contributed to this project, and I am grateful to them all. Let me begin by thanking my family. They have paid the highest price for my passions, preoccupations and absences. First I would like to thank my wife Bette who has graciously tolerated my long-standing enchantment with rivers. She has made numerous float trips with me, has run uncounted shuttles, and has provided the bulk of the photography for all my projects. As my primary proofreader, she is always challenged by the task of transforming my rough manuscripts into "something resembling English." My three children, Erin, Ryan and Kevin, have all shared time on rivers with me, and Kevin seems to have acquired my love of rivers and fishing (and contributed photographs to this book as well).

As I look beyond my family to acknowledge assistance, encouragement and information there are numerous people who should be mentioned. First, without friends who share my enthusiasm for whitewater rivers, I probably never would have become a fanatic. Included here are Richard Johnson, Frank Kennedy, Curt Healey, John Krauss, Jerry Vergamini, Chuck Lienert and Tom Farley. I give special thanks to Dave Parks, an experienced and articulate boatman, who devoted many hours to proofreading and revision of the rough manuscript for this book. Most of what I know about fishing from the bank I learned from my father, Harry, a truly extraordinary steelheader. My early schooling in boat fishing whitewater rivers came from two local commercial guides, C. B. Cummins and Gary Enoch. They are two of the best anywhere, and both willing to answer an endless array of questions. Some other folks instrumental in one way or another to the production of this book are long-time river guide Glen Wooldridge, raft manufacturer Glen Lewman, sportsman Don Dillingham, professional river guide Mary Ann Jones, and publisher Frank Amato whom I especially thank for his time and encouragement.

I need to make some comments regarding the style of the book. Throughout it I have referred to "he," "boatman," "his," and so on. This was done only as a means to ensuring an easily readable text, one not cluttered with "his or her," this or that "person," and the like. Unquestionably the majority of whitewater boatpersons and fisherpersons are male, but there is a significant number of females in both roles. To presume that women cannot excelt in either is both sexist and absurd—there are too many examples to the contrary.

Any book dealing with whitewater river running seems to focus a lot of attention on the dangers of the sport, and this one is no exception. In order to ensure safe floating you need to know what kinds of problems you may face and how to avoid them. I've logged a lot of time on rivers and have yet to find myself in a life-threatening situation. The same is true for virtually every river runner I talk to. I think this is the case for us for two reasons—first, we have learned everything we could and practiced boating skills for years as a hedge against disaster, and second, we are very careful and usually do not extend ourselves beyond common sense and good judgement. Approach your river running in the same way and you're in for years of great enjoyment!

Ray Miskimins

Dedication

For Bette
A Protector of the Earth
and
Erin, Ryan, Kevin
Who Have Followed Her Lead

river run

a downstream float, a loss of time
atop the river that gently flows,
soaking sun, the world will blur
minutes are hours in sweet repose

blue-green water, softly rippling
cascade of crystal upon the ear
without reality, an anesthetic
sense of calm and connection clear

then like a knife, through mind's fog
a distant drum has come to sound,
awake, alert, that's the call
the heart and lungs begin to pound

beyond the boat, a mist arises
and forms a line to end the flat,
there's the lip, disaster's drop
it's time, it's time, to take the mat

over the edge, swallow a breath
the challenge has now begun,
pull to the left, then back to the right
rock, water and light perceptually run

coiled and striking, intense in focus
while seconds seem like days,
then down below, comes clear and smooth
a gradual diminishment of waves

pull up the oars, breathe long and deep
another test is now behind
river of dark, river of light
time to reflect, pause and unwind

a float downstream, taken in sum
earth, heaven and hell are here,
the river's moods, its steady beat
for all of life it forms a mirror

r. w. miskimins

Chapter 1

Introduction

THERE ARE VERY FEW ACTIVITIES THAT OFFER THE excitement and exhilaration you'll experience riding a boat through the rolling waves and frothing foam of whitewater—nature in one of its purest, most powerful and beautiful forms! Rivers have long held a tremendous fascination for mankind. Unlike ponds and lakes and other captured bodies of water, rivers seem to be restless, to breathe, to be alive. They are going somewhere, and they invite you to climb aboard and travel with them.

The whitewater encounter: This is where it all begins. (Courtesy of Whitewater Manufacturing, Grants Pass, Oregon)

Floating Whitewater Rivers

There are some rivers that offer long floats of uninterrupted calm, especially very large ones like the Mississippi or the Columbia. They take on a utilitarian aspect and have been widely used for transport of goods from one town to another. But among rivers they are the exception, for most are smaller, faster, and choked with boulders, narrow passages and other hazards. When the river encounters something that interrupts its smooth and orderly journey, it reacts by creating cushions, holes, waves, chutes, and eddies—areas of swirling, aerated, disturbed water flow that are all captured under the term "whitewater." A definable section of whitewater river between two calm areas is called a rapid, a fitting label that denotes the feeling of high energy created by the crashing currents and rolling waves.

One of the fastest growing sports in the United States in the last decade is river running. Tens of thousands of new people each year have discovered the thrill of floating whitewater. It's a virtually indescribable high! And interspersed among rapids are stretches of peaceful and placid water—time to enjoy the river in a different way, relaxed and calm. A float experience can have many and varied facets: A confrontation with the elements; an intimate place to deepen a friendship; a moving view of a wilderness landscape; a personal challenge, a place to encounter fear; a group of people working as a team; a great suntan; or just a way to divert your attention from the pressures and stresses of everyday life.

Like most people, I can still remember my first whitewater experience. Several years ago a man I worked with, Richard Johnson, invited me and my family for a day trip on the middle Rogue River. His credentials were good; he had spent his summers as a licensed commercial guide on the Wild and Scenic lower section of the Rogue for the last seven years. I'll probably never recapture that feeling I experienced as we went through the first rapid (Dunn Riffle, intermediate class water)—a mixture of curiosity and fear, confusion and excitement. For him it was like a walk in the park. For me, there was no rhyme or reason to the currents, drops, holes and waves that made up the whitewater; and what our boatman was doing with his raft, by pulling and pushing his oars, made even less sense.

After a few hours of floating I began to relax and to feel in harmony with the river. The river took on a structure and a rhythm, one I could liken to music. At times there was a quiet, a calm, like violins softly sounding; at other times you could feel the brass section blaring and the percussion pounding; and there was every kind of ambiance in between the two extremes. It was spectacular!

It was during this trip I first had an opportunity to handle the oars myself. That too was quite an experience. After exchanging seats with Richard I gripped the sticks. Entering the rapid, as the water picked up speed, my instructions were: "Point at what you don't want to hit and pull away from it." This counsel was totally useless to me, and in my confusion I randomly stroked the water with sometimes one, sometimes two oars, and made one of the worst runs ever recorded through an easy rapid called Chair Riffle. Sideways, almost backwards, and finally hitting the bank at the turn I gave up the oars; but at that moment I knew that I was hooked. It was only a matter of time until I got my own boat, found some beginner whitewater, and began to learn how to row.

Until the last decade, river running was primarily a spectator sport. Other than a handful of hard-shell kayakers and about an equal number of boatmen for rafts, most people who encountered whitewater were paying customers for commercially operated float trips. Of course, there are those people who have limited access,

Poor judgement or poor preparation can lead to river mishaps.

funds, time or inclination to run rivers without benefit of guides. Taking a ride with someone else is great fun, but for many of us it is far surpassed by piloting our own craft. Over the past few years the number of do-it-yourself whitewater enthusiasts has increased greater than twenty-fold—there are now likely more than a million people on our nation's rivers each summer. Reflecting this boom in self-sufficient floating, a large percentage of the commercial guiding companies now offer trips where they provide the boats, gear and food, and teach you how to row or paddle your own way down the river.

If you are joining the swelling ranks of whitewater river runners you can look forward to some real thrills. But always remember, a major aspect of the experience that contributes to the excitement is the inherent danger. Regretably, each year a few floaters die on whitewater rivers, and many more are involved in mishaps that leave them injured or frightened of further boating. A large number of people just don't take the river and its perils seriously. For some, it's a kind of "macho" routine, to prove that they are river runner versions of John Wayne; for others, the "splash and giggle set," they enjoy a combination of water, sun and beer, and mindlessly assume that they will make it from put-in to take-out with very little knowledge, caution, or ability for dealing with whitewater. Anyone who has spent a lot of hours floating has encountered these folks, and from time to time pulled them coughing and sputtering out of the water. The last float I was on prior to this writing, I was called upon to transport a 17-year-old girl with a dislocated shoulder to the nearest town. Drinking too much, she had nonchalantly entered an intermediate class rapid in a half-deflated inflatable kayak. Her life jacket was laying in the bottom of the boat. Thrown out of her craft when she went over a drop sideways, she banged into several boulders, dislocated her shoulder, and then nearly drowned.

Later in this book, issues of safety such as use of life jackets and unplanned swims will be covered in detail. Read them carefully. But the first and most important rule will be stated here: Don't take on more than you can handle! Recognize that successfully negotiating whitewater rapids should not be left to luck. There is skill, ability, knowledge, and practice involved. Start with easy floats, get help from those more experienced, work at procedures and techniques like your life depends on it (it does), and only gradually move up to tougher water. Learn the skills involved in controlling your craft, develop the ability to read water, always attend to issues of safety, and study maps, guidebooks, and instructional materials. Trust your judgement on any float—if the water looks like more than you can handle, pull your boat over and scout it carefully. If you still have serious doubts, don't run it!

_____ # Chapter 2

Inflatable Rafts

RAFTS FOR RIVER RUNNING HAVE BEEN READILY available to the general public for about forty years. At the end of World War II military surplus "life rafts" were in abundance. Typically, they were constructed entirely of rubber and designed primarily to be used as lifeboats in emergencies on the high seas. The whitewater raft has undergone a number of very significant transformations since those days.

Materials

The material used to construct present-day craft generally consists of two components: Coating and fabric. The very cheap rafts on the market are usually unreinforced polyvinyl chloride (PVC) or rubberized canvas. In quality rafts, the *fabric* is usually woven nylon or knitted polyester. Fabric strength varies considerably and may be described in one of two ways—fabric weight (ounces per square yard) or thread weight ("denier," a measurement of the coarseness of the thread reflected in grams per 9000 meters of length). There are four common *coatings:* EPDM (a synthetic rubber), neoprene, hypalon, or PVC. Most nylon fabrics are coupled with EPDM, neoprene, or hypalon. EPDM is the least expensive, hypalon the most expensive. For the extra expense the hypalon raft is more abrasion resistant, lighter in weight, and more resistant to deterioration caused by ultraviolet radiation. Typically, knitted polyester is combined with a PVC coating—this combination is usually stiffer and tougher than any of the nylon coated materials and equally resistant to UV rays. As mentioned earlier, the cheap discount store craft are often sloppily constructed of unreinforced or barely reinforced PVC. This has tended to give PVC a bad reputation, one which should be ignored when looking at quality rafts.

Looking through the major manufacturers of top-line craft, there are a number of options in material for the consumer. Udisco and HBIE (Wind River) market EPDM boats with fabrics ranging from 420 denier to 840 denier. Achilles, Avon, Riken (Campways), Rogue Inflatables, and Udisco all manufacture rafts using a hypalon coating (varying from 25% to 80% hypalon), with fabrics ranging from 420 denier to 1260 denier. Maravia and Sotar (Whitewater Manufacturing) market rafts made from a knitted polyester/PVC coating combination.

Commercial whitewater trip in a large hypalon and nylon boat. (Courtesy of Mike Knox)

For some specific examples, the popular Campways River Rider tubes are 420 denier nylon, 25% hypalon (mixed with neoprene) coated; the floor is a heavier 1200 denier fabric. Avon's boats use the same material for tubes and floor, an 80% hypalon and 840 denier fabric. Sotar raft tubes are constructed of 32 ounce knitted polyester, coated with PVC; the floor is 50 ounce fabric. The HBIE "ten-man," a big seller among economy priced rafts, is constructed of 840 denier nylon coated with 100% EPDM. The characteristics of the various materials, the rafter's budget, and local availability generally dictate an individual's choice among the alternatives in raft materials. But, except for occasional playing in lakes and ponds, steer clear of the cheapies—they often prove to be much more expensive in the long run.

Design

In addition to the materials employed, there have been many design and construction changes since the old rubber lifeboat. Stability is the only positive feature of the World War II vintage craft. A raft for running whitewater rivers must not only be stable, but as important, it must maneuverable. The most notable difference when comparing old and new boats is the upturned bow and stern of the newer craft. For medium sized craft, the bow and stern typically raise about 10 or 11 inches. The upturned ends cut down the amount of raft touching the water, allowing for easier pivoting; the upturned stern reduces the current's resistance to back ferrying, the primary type of rowing for oared rafts; the upturned bow deflects water from splashing into the boat and makes for a smoother ride over big waves.

Modern Whitewater Raft

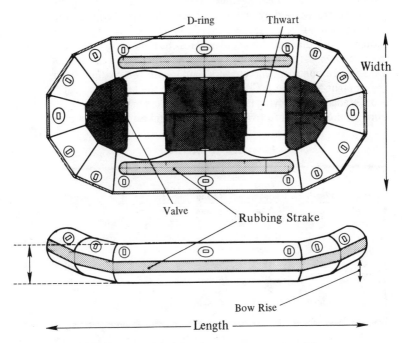

Before selecting a raft and sorting through a number of other design features you must make two critical decisions: The size of boat you want, and whether you will row or paddle it. *Raft sizes* are best considered by length and width (and secondarily, tube diameter). There exists a long-standing system still applied to many rafts, especially the smaller ones, based upon how many people can be packed into it in an emergency on the ocean. When running whitewater rivers, a ten-man raft used with oars will hold 3 or 4 people (including the boatman), and when used as a paddle boat it will comfortably hold 5 or 6. I row a ten-man raft; for an afternoon suntan float through town I've had as many as six on the boat, but on big water and carrying a lot of gear for camping, two passengers are plenty. Two issues must be considered when loading passengers and gear: Space and flotation. Regarding the latter, many whitewater raft manufacturing companies have been increasing their tube diameters over the past several years to accommodate the overloading in weight that plagues boaters doing multi-day floats.

The chart of raft sizes gives common boat dimensions starting with the "rubber duckies," up to the very large "class VI" rafts (18 feet or more in length). This chart does not include the giant multi-tube rafts and tied-together combinations of rafts and pontoons sometimes used by commercial outfitters (primarily on the Colorado River)—some of these exceed 30 feet and are powered by motors rather than oars or paddles. Most beginner and intermediate boatmen own rafts 14 feet long or less; and there are a number of experienced boatmen who are very happy with the medium-sized six- or eight-man boats. Generally speaking, the larger the boat the more stable and forgiving it is, but it is also less maneuverable, requires more strength to row, and is more cumbersome to transport.

Common Raft Sizes

Length	Width	Tube Diameter	Rating	No. of People Rowed	No. of People Paddled
7½'	4½'	12"	2-man	1	1
10'	5'	14"	4-man	1	2
12'	6'	15"	6-man	2-3	3-4
12½'	6'	16"	8-man	3	4
14'	6½'	18"	10-man	3-4	5-6
15½'	7'	20"	14-man	4	6
16'	7½'	22"	16-man	4-5	7-8
18'	8'	24"	18-man	5	9

Beyond the factor of size of your boat and how it will be propelled, there are a number of other details to consider. Most medium-size craft have two thwarts, either permanently installed or removable (held in with velcro or with lacing). Thwarts are inflated cross-tubes inside the raft, near the bow and stern. They provide a little additional flotation, but their main function is to provide stiffness and consistent shape to the boat. If you use a rowing frame it will accomplish the same thing, so many oarsmen remove one or both of them.

Most rafts, except the cheapies, have four inflatable chambers (in addition to the two thwarts). The multiple chambers add a safety factor should the boat material be ripped. There is some variation in valves used. Most popular are the one-inch military type, and they can vary from cheap iron castings to finely finished hi-tech aluminum. A few manufacturers offer well-engineered modern versions of the old plastic push-lock valves. Another feature to look for is reinforcement in potential areas of wear. Most common and important are rubbing strakes (added overlapping material) around the midpoint of the outside of the tubes and along the side tubes on top. The latter is particularly important if you are going to use a rowing frame. Also, consider the number, placement, and quality of attached D-rings. These rings are important for attaching anything to your boat, from a rowing frame to gear to a bow line.

Large paddle raft in Class IV whitewater.

An area of particular concern in designing whitewater boats is the *raft floor*. The most common injury to rafts is tearing of the floor material—it is often subjected to abuse from rocks. A number of manufacturers have greatly increased the weight of the fabric used for their floors. Some wrap the floor up to the outside midline of the boat to afford added protection to the bottom and lower sides of the tubes. A very recent development has been the self-bailing floor. Imagine an air mattress laced into the bottom of a boat and that's essentially what they look like. Water inside the raft simply runs out around the laced-together seam. They add flotation, eliminate bailing (and thus, taking on considerable weight in big rapids), and tend to stiffen the boat. By avoiding turning your raft into a bathtub, it maintains its maneuverability when waves are crashing over the tubes. Stiffening it and adding flotation also adds to maneuverability and makes wrapping around rocks less likely. The only possible negative factor for self-bailing boats is an increased susceptibility to flipping—they don't bend with holes and waves quite as readily as rafts with conventional floors.

Rafts vary considerably in quality of construction. They are made by hand from a large number of pieces of material. One can expect some variation from one to the next because of the human factor in construction. However, cheaper rafts can be identified readily just by checking the seams. Seams should be heavy, smooth, straight, wide, and well overlapped. You need only put a few rafts of varying quality side-by-side to rapidly become an expert on quality of construction.

Accessories

Once you have decided on a boat—based upon whether you wish to paddle or row and how much weight you want to carry, and taking into account issues of design and quality of construction—you now need to equip your craft. Minimally, you need paddles, and if you are going to row you need a frame and oars.

Raft Frames

The majority of commercial outfitters and serious rafters prefer rowing to paddling. It puts the control of the boat into one pair of hands. The frame serves several functions, most importantly providing a rigid base for attaching oarlocks, seats and a floor. Years ago, virtually all of them were made from wood; now most frames are made from metal. On rare occasion, you'll see one made from plastic pipe, fiberglass, or other materials, but these frames have yet to be proven as to strength and durability. The premium frames are constructed of aluminum because it is strong, lightweight, and maintenance free. I have built rowing frames of wood, steel, and aluminum and seen them all go into extended big water trips. They all work, but the limited life of wood and weight and upkeep with steel are significant disadvantages.

A rowing frame is made to the exact specifications of a particular raft, and essentially begins with long sections of wood or metal on both sides of the raft (they lay lengthwise on top the main tubes). A pair of cross supports are placed at each end of the long sections,

Aluminum raft frame designed and built at the Rogue River Boat Shop, Grants Pass, Oregon.

seat is attached to the front cross supports, and a seat for the boat-man is attached to the rear cross supports. Oarstands to hold the oarlocks (or pins) are affixed to the frame above the main tubes just forward of the boatman's seat. For metal frames, if you want to add a rigid (usually marine plywood) floor, then several drops are welded to the underside of the frame. Metal strips to bolt on the plywood are welded to the bottom of the drops. If you have a frame with a rigid floor, consider putting a large sheet of two-inch-thick closed cell foam underneath it. The foam will protect the floor of your raft

Floating Whitewater Rivers

running parallel to and usually directly over the thwarts. A passenger when bouncing over rocks (the floor material can't get caught between two rigid objects, the frame floor and a rock). As a nice secondary benefit, the foam adds rigidity and flotation to your boat. With or without a floor, quality frames provide a foot brace of some kind—something stable to place your feet on when you need to pull hard on the oars. When finished, the rowing frame is strapped (one- to two-inch-wide nylon straps) to four to six of the D-rings on the outside of your raft.

Raft Frame (Rear Thwart Removed)

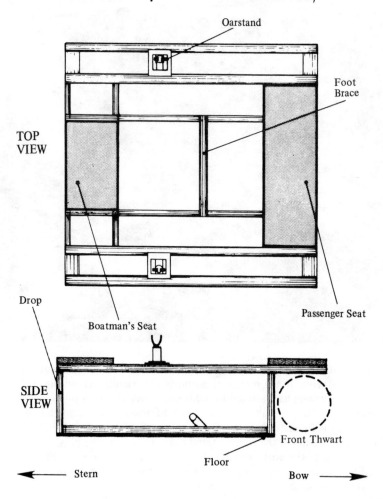

Oarstand

Foot Brace

TOP VIEW

Passenger Seat

Drop

Boatman's Seat

SIDE VIEW

Front Thwart

Floor

← Stern

Bow →

There are various options and refinements available for frames, depending upon the manufacturer. Often they design into the frame an ice chest which serves as the boatman's seat or is underneath the seat; in either case the rear thwart must be removed. Some companies provide a dry box (watertight storage compartment) as the front seat. In this design the front thwart is removed. When a frame is used, removal of one or both thwarts is not a problem—the frame more than adequately substitutes for the thwarts in maintaining the shape of the raft. Other frame options include cold drink receptacles, rope or padded seat(s), hinged boatman seat (for access to a cooler underneath), small trays, attached bilge pumps (for removal of water inside the boat), special attachments to hold more ice chests (behind the passenger's seat or alongside of them), a gear deck (rigid, angled floor behind the boatman), and so on. For those rafters who do not own a trailer to haul their raft and frame assembled and ready to slide into the water, some manufacturers offer frames that come apart into several smaller, more manageable sections.

Oarlocks, Oars and Paddles

If you intend to paddle your raft you will need to invest in some *paddles*. There are two decisions to make: Length and materials. Rafters use paddles in the four- to six-foot range, depending on the size of the tubes they are sitting on and the paddler's size. To measure yourself for a paddle, with the boat in the water sit on a side tube and reach out and take a stroke. When the blade is fully into the water, the top of the paddle should be at chin to nose height. If you are uncertain, go a few inches longer rather than shorter. Commercial outfitters find that a 60-inch paddle will fit most full-size adults. The paddle captain (the person sitting on the stern) usually will want an additional six or eight inches in length to increase the sweep of his ruddering-style strokes.

Paddles are constructed either of wood or of metal and plastic. Some of the top-line wood paddles have synthetic handles (usually "T" shaped) and reinforcement of metal or plastic on the blades. The only disadvantage to good wood paddles is in durability and need for regular maintenance. Some of the aluminum and plastic paddles, while not as aesthetically pleasing, are virtually indestructible.

If your raft is equipped with a rowing frame, you'll need to place either *pins* or *oarlocks* in the oarstands. The pin and clip system consists of a clip mounted to the oar which snaps onto a pin (metal shaft) extending upward out of the oarstand. Most who employ oarlocks use the open ("U" shaped) variety. These have a stem which drops through the top of the oarstand. A cotter pin or split ring is used at the base of the stem to prevent the freely turning oarlock from popping up and out. Depending upon what part of the country you're in or who you talk to, pins and clips or oarlocks are better; however, I suspect that nationwide pins and clips are considerably more popular than oarlocks. Personally, I prefer oarlocks because they allow you to "feather" the blades—with a slight rotation of the wrist you can keep the blade oriented for maximum power throughout the entire stroke. Also, I like the option of nearly two feet of lateral movement they afford (you can pull the handles clear across your body to the opposite tube if you want). You can "finesse" your strokes by changes in both the depth and reach of the blade into the water (a fact that is especially important for whitewater fishing). However, the first time you go for a critical pull and find your blades slicing sideways through the water, you'll see a great advantage to pins and clips—they keep the oars fixed in place. If you use open oarlocks you'll have to learn to approach every rapid with a check on the position of your blades. Also, pins and clips allow greater power to your strokes (especially when using oversize blades) and are less fatiguing to the boatman because you don't have to expend any energy to keep the blades oriented.

No matter what your decision is on oarlocks versus pins and clips, you next have to purchase *oars*. The same two variables that applied to paddles operate here: Length and materials. A good rule of thumb to determine length of oars is to measure from oarlock to oarlock (or pin to pin) and add 50 percent. My ten-man boat frame measures very slightly over six feet from oarlock to oarlock—I use nine-foot oars. You'll have to increase the oar length if your raft tubes are very large. Also, when choosing oars, better a little long than too short. Generally, boats 12 feet long require 7- to 7½-foot oars, 13-foot boats need 8- to 8½-foot oars, 14-foot boats need 9- to 9½-foot oars, and 15-foot craft require 10- or 10½-foot oars.

Oars are available in either wood or metal and plastic. I have both and see the choice as primarily a matter of personal preference. However, it seems clear that the synthetic oars are more durable and their blades come in different sizes and are replaceable. I caught a blade between two rocks in a Class IV rapid—the oarlock bent and the oar flipped out of my hand, landing in the water 30 feet from the boat. I retrieved it downstream and later replaced the blade. A wooden oar in the same predicament likely would have snapped in two. Synthetic oars do vary in flexibility, from very stiff to about the same flexibility as wood. More flexible oars tend to increase stroke power because at the end of a hard pull they literally "snap" back into a straight alignment.

Whatever the material you choose for your oars, if you use oar-locks you will need to protect the oar shaft from excessive wear. I prefer a wrap of 3/16-inch braided nylon cord. Some of the aluminum shafted oars come with a plastic sleeve for protection. For quietness of operation, that sleeve can be wrapped with nylon cord, too. Also with oarlocks, you will need to put on oarstops (large rubber "O" rings) so the oar can't slide through the oarlock and into the water. If your oars are made from wood, you can increase their life by keeping them varnished. For a better grip, do not varnish the handles.

Other Accessories

In a later chapter on river camping, a large number of items useful or necessary to meal preparation and staying overnight will be described. However, there are other fundamental accessories to rafting that every rafter should consider, even for a two-hour afternoon float.

Three types of pumps: 12-volt, barrel,and foot.

Inflatable rafts, by definition, require air to fill the chambers and thwarts. There are three basic kinds of inflators (ruling out your lungs, gas-fueled power blowers, and your home vacuum cleaner with the hose reversed). There are a number of power pumps available, operating on 12-volt battery electricity. Unless you carry a battery on the river, they are useful only at the set-in next to your vehicle. The two kinds of manually operated units are foot pumps and barrel pumps. There are high volume, good quality versions of both, and choice is a matter of personal preference. Be certain that the nozzle of the one you select fits snugly into the type of valve that is on your raft.

Unless you've got the new self-bailing floor in your boat, you'll need some means for removing the water that splashes or pours into it. Some rafters are content with a small plastic bucket or a one-gallon plastic jug with the bottom cut out for bailing. One step up, there are barrel pumps in various sizes for clearing out unwanted water. At the top of the line, there are available frame-mounted manual and 12-volt models, rarely seen except on large commercial boats.

Even if your run is a short one, you will likely have some things you want to be certain will stay dry (like cameras, repair kit, car keys, and so on). There are available a wide variety of waterproof gadget bags and pouches. Extremely popular with rafters are metal ammunition cans—not only are they entirely waterproof, but they are rigid, preventing crushing of the contents. The various options in waterproof containers are related in detail in Chapter VII. There are other items, gear to ensure the safety of life and limb, that you should carry in your raft for use even on day trips. Most significant in this category is the personal flotation device (PFD, or life jacket). PFD's and other important safety accessories will be elaborated upon in Chapter IX, Common Sense and Safety.

While some are fixing dinner is also a good time for others to patch a ripped floor.

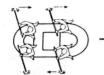 _____ # Chapter 3

Other Whitewater Boats

DURING A FLOAT DOWN A TYPICAL WHITEWATER stretch of river you'll certainly see some rafts. However, you will likely see a number of other kinds of non-motorized craft. Depending on the run's location and the difficulty of the rapids you may see catarafts, inflatable kayaks, hardshell kayaks, canoes, or driftboats—all of these boats are covered below. You may also see inner tubes (singly or several lashed together), wooden rafts, lake-type rowboats, and so on. I never cease to be amazed at what people will climb aboard to float a river.

Inflatable Kayaks/Canoes

On the majority of whitewater rivers, rafts are the boats most often seen. Following in a close second, especially in intermediate class day-trip areas, are elongated inflatable craft designed to accommodate usually one and sometimes two paddlers. They are referred to by many names, most often Tahiti (a registered name), inflatable canoe, or inflatable kayak (a fact which irritates some hardshell kayakers). They typically are 2½ to 3 feet wide, about 10½ feet long for one-man versions and about 12 feet long for two-man boats. Although these craft are far less stable than rafts, they are more maneuverable, more portable, and the boat and gear much less costly. Everyone in my family has one and they are great for those days when you spontaneously decide you feel like running the river for a few hours—throw boat, paddle, PFD, and pump in the car and go. However, they are not toys and can make a trip through Class III or

IV rapids an exciting challenge of your whitewater knowledge and ability. Like any small craft, you trade maneuverability for stability and you need to approach big water accordingly. Several years ago I was playing around in whitewater in a two-man sized Sea Eagle and thought I was pretty skillful at back paddling—they don't do well sideways through holes, at least when compared to my large raft. With inflatable kayaks/canoes you pretty much plan on being upside down occasionally if you run rapids of any size. However, the capsizing and flipping the boat back upright are not nearly as traumatic or problematic as with a large raft.

One-man inflatable kayak in whitewater. (Courtesy of Orange Torpedo Trips, Grants Pass, Oregon)

If you are going to acquire an inflatable kayak/canoe, there are a number of variables similar to choosing a raft that must be considered. Design doesn't vary remarkably, but some have more upturn to the bow or stern, there are different approaches to splash protection, seat construction differs a little, a few boats offer laced-in self-bailing floors, and so on. More critical, check the boat's construction, in particular the materials used. The less expensive (and much less durable) models are made entirely of vinyl, like the cheapest rafts. The topline boats are very neatly constructed from either PVC coated knitted polyester or hypalon coated woven nylon, like the best quality rafts (see the section in Chapter II on raft materials). Also, examine the valves; they are often a problem for otherwise well-made boats. Finally, you will need a pump, maybe some waterproof containers, and a paddle, preferably the two-bladed type used by hard-shell kayakers (described later).

Catarafts

Imagine a rowing frame perched atop two long pontoons and you have a cataraft. Their two greatest claims to fame are that without a floor or inner compartment they effectively are self-bailing, and they generally cannot be tilted on edge and wrapped against a rock. Their drawbacks are a reduction in space for gear and increased difficulty in rowing (more specifically, in turning the boat to angle across the river). I built a one-man cataraft that I've dubbed "mini-cat," with 11-foot-long, 12-inch-diameter tubes. It's a lively, highly maneuverable, low-riding, wet little boat. However, most catarafts are large to very large, designed to hold four or more people. The long, inflatable tubes generally range in length up to 18 feet, with diameters from 18 to 30 inches. They are made from the same materials as rafts (see Chapter II). Occasionally you will see a cataraft with three, four or five tubes instead of just two. Adding pontoons increases the flotation for carrying a lot of weight. The frames for catarafts are very similar to those for rafts and can be made from wood, steel, or aluminum (see raft frames, Chapter II).

The mini-cat, a small one-man cataraft.

Kayaks

There are three main kinds of "hard boats" frequently found floating whitewater rivers (excluding the various kinds of powerboats seen primarily on the milder sections): kayaks, canoes and drift boats. They all are typically constructed from fiberglass, plastic, aluminum or wood. Kayaks and canoes, as compared to small inflatable craft, are much more maneuverable but usually not as stable. Drift boats are easier to handle than comparable sized rafts and nearly as stable. Considering all three, the hard boats are a lot less forgiving—they don't readily ignore all the mistakes that inflatables will (like hitting rocks, floating into holes sideways, bumping other boats, taking on water, and so on).

Whitewater acrobatics in a hard-shell kayak. (Courtesy of Chuck Schlumpberger)

The sports car of the river is the one-man, hard-shell kayak. These kayaks are the only whitewater craft regularly seen in international maneuverability and speed competition. There also exist two-man kayaks and decked canoes (paddler kneels rather than sits), but they are less frequently seen on our nation's whitewater rivers. There also are available "touring" kayaks, designed for flatwater (lakes, bays, and so on). They are long (generally 16 or 17 feet), flat, stable and constructed to track easily. Whitewater kayaks are generally short with considerable rocker (the curvature of the bottom from end to end). With a short boat, the strong curve of the bottom, and the fact that there's no keel, the whitewater kayak is extremely maneuverable and will turn on a dime. However, they can be tricky for beginners to paddle in a straight line or to keep upright through waves and drops.

Kayak Interior Bracing System

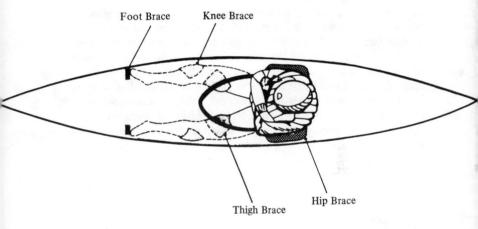

Foot Brace   Knee Brace

Thigh Brace   Hip Brace

Looking inside the whitewater kayak you'll find an elaborate system of bracing. It is important that the boater achieve a snug fit for his rear and legs so that all his bodily motion is directly transferred to the boat (however, not so tight that exit is a problem in an emergency). Mounted inside the boat should be foot, knee, thigh, hip and back braces and a seat. All these can be adjusted by adding or subtracting from the closed cell foam, plastic, or fiberglass used to make the braces.

31

The shells of whitewater kayaks are made either from fiberglass (for example, Kevlar or E glass) or molded polyethylene plastic. They range in length from about 11 to 13 feet, and are around 2 feet wide. The shorter versions have been dubbed "play boats" because of their increased maneuverability and suitability for "hot dogging" (techniques like endos, rolls, hole-rides, and pirouettes). Some kayaks have a particularly low-cut cockpit; this can increase the boater's mobility for leaning and bracing. All whitewater kayaks have an extended lip all around the cockpit. The lip is for attaching the spray skirt that is around the kayaker's waist—this keeps the boat interior airtight and dry.

In addition to a spray skirt, helmet, and PFD (the latter two are covered later under issues of safety), you'll need a paddle and some waterproof clothing (like a wetsuit). Whitewater kayak paddles range in length from about 72 inches to 84 inches (flatwater touring kayakers generally use paddles in the 90 to 96 inch range). They consist of a long shaft, about 1½ inches in diameter, with a blade at both ends. As was the case for rafting paddles and oars, kayak paddles are available in both wood and synthetics, the latter considerably more popular (and more durable). Some paddles come apart in the middle for easier transport to and from the river. Most have feathered blades (the blades are set at right angles to one another), but the ones that break down can usually be set feathered or non-feathered. For most kayakers, feathered blades are more comfortable, especially when alternating their strokes on both sides of the boat or doing rolls. Finally, blade shapes, curvature, and sizes vary from one model to the next, and should be chosen based upon personal preferences and style of boating.

Canoes

Open canoes are seen more and more often on our whitewater rivers, especially on the milder stretches. For years they have enjoyed greater popularity in the East than in the West. They were originally designed for flat water, with little or no built-in flotation and were very tenuous (unstable) in waves. However, they tracked across lakes and up calm rivers with amazing ease. There now are canoes specially designed for heavy whitewater. The keel has been altered, the bow profile changed, the sides are higher, and flotation bags of foam come with them. Despite these modifications they still require considerable skill to keep upright in big water. A large number of design aspects of canoes vary from one to the next but any increase in maneuverability has to give up some ease of tracking and stability —there is no perfect all-purpose boat, so buy the one that best fits your intended use. The paddles for canoeing are those that were described for paddle rafting (see Chapter II).

Open canoe in whitewater. (Courtesy of Beaver Creek Lodge, Klamath River, California)

Drift Boats

The boat of choice on whitewater fishing rivers in the West has for years been the drift boat. Rowboats of various designs were available long before any inflatable raft, and some of them were used by miners or trappers or fishermen or others to float down rivers with whitewater rapids. Modern drift boats are technically built in a "dory" design, modified versions of the New England rowboats used by whalers when setting off from the much larger mother ship. The basic dory design—flat bottomed, sides flared, and pointed on both ends—can be traced back to the Phoenicians on the Mediterranean. These craft may be constructed from wood, fiberglass, or aluminum (the latter generally considered the lightest, most durable and maintenance free). Most of the ones we see on our nation's rivers are the McKenzie style—this design is characterized by more rocker, a wider bottom, and higher and more flared sides (especially in front) when

Drift boats are ideally suited to fishing whitewater rivers.

compared to the old-style rowboat. Driftboats are about 15 feet long, 6½ feet wide at the top, 4½ feet wide at the bottom.

Above all, drift boats are dry and comfortable, and particularly suited to whitewater fishing (see Chapter VIII). The boat I own has swivel chairs up front for the passengers, a rope seat for me, large airtight storage, an 11,000 BTU heater, shelved storage area under the bow, and so on. Drift boat oars are the same as those used for rafts (refer to the section in Chapter II on oars). The boats of modern design are extremely maneuverable and capable of running up to Class IV+ rapids with amazing ease. Just don't make any mistakes —the materials used to construct these craft and their lack of built-in flotation can render them unforgiving in time of trouble. The Sheriff in charge of marine patrol on the Rogue River in Oregon recently stated that literally dozens of drift boats are lost at Blossom Bar Rapids alone each year! There are available some dories particularly designed for very heavy whitewater. They are generally constructed of fiberglass or molded plastic with large integral flotation and storage chambers. Unlike the standard McKenzie boat, they won't sink when tipped or swamped.

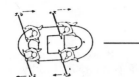 **Chapter 4**

Reading the River

MOST WHITEWATER ENTHUSIASTS BEGIN EITHER BY traversing a route they see others take through a rapid, or by closing their eyes and putting trust in the inherent forgiveness of inflatable craft. I have seen literally hundreds of runs through rapids where people trusted too much to luck—for a few it caught up with them, resulting in disaster. You may think someone is pulling your leg if they say you've got to learn to "read the river," but that expression denotes something very serious. The only way you can safely negotiate a whitewater river is to be able to know what's coming, and then properly control your craft in light of that knowledge. For most people, rowing or paddling quickly becomes easy, but learning to discern what's ahead can take a lifetime. To perceive and actually understand the hydraulics and hazards of a rapid is captured under the phrase "reading the river."

In Grants Pass, Oregon, there is a man named Glen Wooldridge who has spent over a half-century floating whitewater rivers. He began in 1915, long before it was fashionable, and has been called the "Dean of Whitewater Boatmen." As a commercial fishing guide he hosted the likes of Zane Grey, Clark Gable, Herbert Hoover, and Ginger Rogers. A boatman who "craved fast water like a steelhead," he discovered that "the best education a whitewater man could have" was learning to read the water. In a recent conversation I asked Glen how one goes about acquiring this skill. He replied: "That's a very difficult thing to do . . . it's hard to explain because there are so many different versions and different types of water. It just takes experience." In his biography, *A River to Run* (written by Florence Arman), he related some thoughts about this complicated subject.

"There are several things about the water that tell you what is going on underneath, where the danger is. The color of the water, its motion, density, and sounds all tell you part of the story. You have to pay close attention to them, because your life and the others in the boat all depend on it. There will be black, slick places; frothy whitewater; more dense whitewater; rapids; riffles; currents; falls; swirls and eddies; chutes and bends. Slick, glassy water is sometimes

Floating Whitewater Rivers

dead water, but at other times it is swift rapids. It takes an experienced riverman to tell the difference before he gets into it. Frothy whitewater is full of air caused by the pounding of the water over a riverbed full of boulders. It is thin water and can't be run. Whitewater that is more dense is over deeper boulders and you can run it. Fast, smooth water is deep and navigable. You can tell the depth of a boulder under fast-moving water by the motion of the water over it. The wake of the water, over the boulder, tells its position underneath the surface. A wave doesn't necessarily mean rocks; it can be just the speed of the river's current. Decisions must be made fast and constantly as to which whitewater is runnable. There isn't always a clear, open channel to follow."

Rock-infested fast water often requires several course changes to assure safe passage.

The river operates by gravity—water flows from a higher point to a lower one within the boundaries established by its bottom and banks. If the bottom was always smooth, the slope gradual and even, and the banks high and wide, there would be no rapids (like concrete irrigation channels, for example). Thankfully, nature does not provide clear channels and steady slope for most of our rivers. Whitewater is created by abrupt changes in elevation (known as drops), narrowing banks, boulders on the bottom, rock ledges, and so on. Your basic goal as you enter any section of whitewater is to reach the end of it with you, your boat, passengers and gear intact—right side up and safe. To do that you must learn to identify and then avoid or properly negotiate all the various obstacles a rapid can throw at you.

Scouting

Prior to running any rapid you need to study it. For minor whitewater with few and very obvious obstacles you can do that as you float up to it in your boat. Often you'll see a raft's boatman stand up just prior to a Class I or II riffle; you can see a little better standing up. For major rapids, especially one you've never seen before, or one with a large drop or sharp turn which makes it impossible to see the turmoil below from your boat, or one which can entrap boats (presenting another obstacle for those following), it's wise to pull over to the shore before running it. Even on rapids scouted and run previously, with any notable change in water level they should be re-scouted. Hike downstream along the bank until you are in a position to see the entire rapid. Standing on firm ground you can study the whitewater, ponder various routes through it, consult with others, and so on. If you check out a river from the road (often done as part of shuttling) be aware that you may miss some rapids and that from a long distance above you often cannot be very accurate in your assessments.

Take your time when scouting and start by getting the broad picture: How long is the rapid, where does it bend or turn, what is the speed of the water, where are the major eddies, what are the main hazards? Develop a mental image of the entire rapid, especially long, rocky ones (you may need it desperately later). Following your general look, starting with the entry, plan each maneuver you will need to complete the run—mentally pick your way through, identifying critical points and critical moves. When you've done that, and you commit to running the rapid, go for it! Overscouting can result in wavering decisions and too much tension. When you are in the whitewater, unless you've made a serious error in your scouting, stick to your plan. However, if you have to make a change at one point, chances are good that you can immediately return to your original route after completing the altered maneuver.

Sometimes when you scout you may determine that a rapid is more than you can handle. If you are in your boat, in midstream, it is likely too late to do anything but run it, whatever the consequences. When scouting from the shore you can choose to line (send your boat through unmanned, guided by ropes held by people on the shore) or portage (carry your boat and gear along the bank until you get past the whitewater). Always when there is any doubt, take the time to stop and scout to see what kind of a mess you're getting into downstream. Scouting is fundamental and essential to safe whitewater floating.

Entry

In bigger rapids, usually the most critical move you'll make is the entry. Before beginning a stretch of whitewater, it is important to look at the whole rapid to avoid having to make lengthy lateral moves. In contrast to the ease of movement in calm water, moving sideways across the river in a rapid is hampered by the increased water speed, by rocks, by shallow areas, and by waves and other kinds of turbulence.

A *tongue* (also called slot), a "V" with the base or point downstream, indicates a passageway between two obstacles. The top of the "V" is where the smooth flow of the river has been interrupted,

Downstream V (Tongue) and Upstream V (Obstacle)

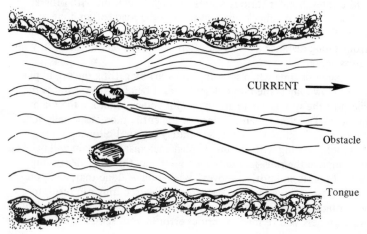

CURRENT ⟶

Obstacle

Tongue

usually by rocks. Obviously, you would like to avoid the rocks, so pass between them. Usually a large tongue provides the safest entry to any rapid. If you look at a long, rocky rapid, you'll likely see several tongues throughout its length. Mid-rapid tongues are sometimes difficult to see after you make your entry because of the turbulence of the water—there is not an experienced boatman alive who has not been at one time or another surprised by a hazard encountered in the midst of roily water. Generally, for the correct route through a rapid, your boat enters via a tongue and then slips through several more to complete the run.

Examination of a rapids will show you that in addition to the "V's" with the base downstream, there are also "V's" with the base upstream. This second kind of "V" indicates an obstacle. The river flow has been interrupted, usually by a rock, and the water fans out downstream on both sides of it—the obstacle is the point or base of the "V."

Safe entry to this Class III drop is the tongue just off the left bank and through the tailwaves that follow it.

Tailout

At the base of a rapid there typically exists a series of waves, varying in height dependent upon the amount of drop and the obstacles the river flow encountered, and caused by fast water meeting slower water. These waves are referred to as *tailwaves*, and if very large, some boaters call them standing waves or haystacks. These waves, collectively known as the tailout, are usually quite regular, obstacle-free, and safe. They give boaters an exciting roller coaster ride out of the whitewater. Tailwaves are a special favorite of kayakers; they can achieve a kind of equilibrium moving laterally called "surfing." Smaller craft do need to be wary, however, of very large waves—if you get turned sideways they can flip you.

Eddies

As you look at a rapid, another feature you should be aware of is the eddy. They typically create no danger, but are great places to relax and catch your breath. For novices, they sometimes are places to get momentarily trapped and spun around. Again, that's not dangerous except in the circumstance you would be spun out of control into heavy whitewater or into a hazard. An eddy is a small section of water, most often along the bank or behind large rocks, that is moving in the opposite direction from the main current. Effectively, water is coming upstream to fill gaps left when the river flow was diverted out and around protrusions from the bank or midstream

Eddies: Along the Bank and in Midstream

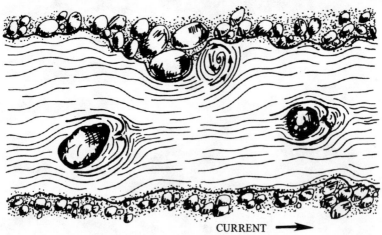

CURRENT ⟶

40

obstacles. The transition area between water flowing upstream and water moving downstream is called the *eddy line.* Whether from the eddy or the main current it is sometimes hard to break through that line, especially with a raft–boaters generally try to build up as much speed as possible before attempting it.

Turns

Rivers flow straight for a while, only to sooner or later turn left or right. Some bends are gentle, barely perceptible, while at the other extreme are sharp "U" or "hairpin" turns. When the river's borders bend, the river is initially inclined to continue going straight. Thus, there is greater force and water speed on the outside of the bend as the river crashes against the outside bank. The inside of the turn is much calmer and slower. However, it is usually shallower too, because the river has cut its main flow channel on the outside and because sediment (sand and rock) is being dropped in the slower current on the inside. This latter fact accounts for the observation that

Near the end of this rapid the river makes a sharp right turn; boatmen have to work hard to avoid being swept into rocks.

Typical Bend in the River

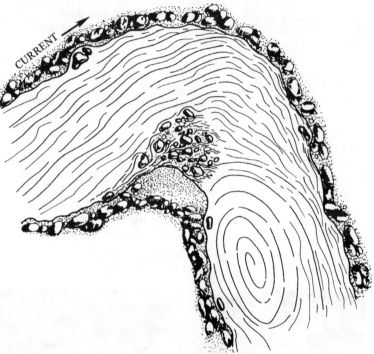

many turns, other than in narrow rock canyons, have sand or gravel bars on the inside of the bend. Most boaters "lean to the inside" on turns, staying in the slower current where obstacles can't pop up very fast. They can always move over into the swifter water on the outside if it is clear and they choose to, but moving from outside to inside is a much tougher feat.

Narrows

The width of the banks of a river obviously do not remain constant. In the wider sections, if there are no obstacles to divert the river flow, the water runs slowly and smoothly. If the banks narrow substantially, the current will pick up speed through the constriction. Some of the most exciting rapids are formed by three features occurring in the same area: Substantial drop in elevation, large rocks in midstream, and a narrow canyon. Below a narrow section where the water begins slowing down, often a series of waves will occur, forming a tailout. A great roller coaster ride may be available.

An interesting kind of hydraulic can be formed in narrows where the water is very deep and the canyon walls very uneven. This combination can produce a churning, swirling, boiling mass of whitewater as great volumes of water are battling with constricted space. A good example of this is the "Coffee Pot" on the Rogue River in Oregon; aptly named, sometimes boats are thrashed helplessly about in there for five or ten minutes.

Coffeepot Rapid in Mule Creek Canyon on the Rogue River: A narrow, deep section of churning whitewater.

Rocks

Generally speaking, rocks are usually the whitewater floater's number one concern. You must be concerned not only about the ones you can see, but also those just below the surface that you can't see. The two kinds present different problems and are discussed in the two sections following.

Above the Surface

Many rivers have lots of rocks protruding above the surface of the water. They only present a problem when you have to work to avoid hitting them. In fast water, often they are directly in your path. Obviously, a boatman should make very effort not to hit rocks. At the least, the collision may spin the boat around; at the most, current pressure pounding the rock may wash an inflatable up on its side against the rock and hold it there. Hitting a large rock sideways in heavy current, the upstream side tube can be forced down, the downstream side tube goes up, and then the river force against the floor of the boat wraps it around the rock. In heavy current it may require cutting out the floor and hours of hard work with ropes from other rocks or the shore to free a large raft. Wrapping and unwrapping inflatables is covered in detail in Chapter IX, Common Sense and Safety. Water piles up on the upstream side of a rock above the surface, forming a *cushion*. Many a threatened wrap has been saved by this cushion. However, the cushion works best on your behalf only when you hit it head on.

Raft encountering a cushion on the upstream side of a boulder.

Rock Above the Surface

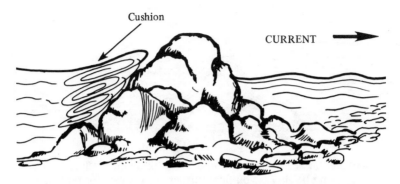

Cushion

CURRENT →

There are some occasions when you cannot avoid hitting a rock. I once was moving rapidly down a narrow chute on the Klamath River in California and realized that due to the unusually low water level there were three rocks sticking out I had never seen before. They were strategically placed with insufficient space for a large raft to float straight between them. I chose to plow head-on into the middle one (which was also slightly more upstream), then take a stroke to swing the stern right to do a 180 around the rock and drop through a tongue. Sometimes in tight spots with unavoidable rocks, you'll want to hit them stern first so that when you're spun around you'll be oriented with your bow headed downstream. Any rapid requiring that level of finesse should be carefully scouted from the shore by boatmen who are adept both at reading the river and controlling their craft.

Below the Surface

As we consider rocks below the surface of the water, differentiate those buried fairly deep as compared to rocks just barely covered. If a boulder sits on the bottom in very slow, deep water there will be little or no perceptible indications on the surface. However, if it's a foot or two from the top or the water is very fast two hydraulic features will result. There may be a slight rise directly over the rock, a *pillow*, and downstream from it some waves. If you encounter waves in a stretch of water for no obvious reason (like a visible obstacle or a narrowing of the river bank), there's probably a large rock well below the surface. Often the pillow is not evident. The surface waves are formed by subsurface water rising up and over a rock, then dropping rapidly over the downstream face of the boulder, hitting the river bottom, then shooting back up. Each successive wave is

45

Rock Well Below the Surface

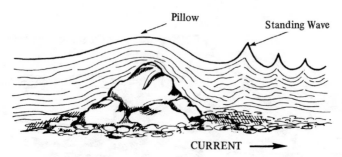

Pillow

Standing Wave

CURRENT ⟶

essentially the same phenomenon of water rising then falling, losing energy (wave height) as you float further downstream for the original rise and drop.

Rocks well under the surface of the water typically create no difficulties. At the most they create relatively harmless standing waves downstream. But a rock just below the surface can present a definite hazard. As described for well-covered rocks, there is a rise and fall hydraulic, but now a potentially dangerous one. There will be a smooth bump (pillow) formed as the water rises to pass over the rock. Sometimes, dependent upon the rock shape and depth and water speed, a "rooster tail" (near vertical spray off the front of the rock) may be created. If you pass directly over the pillow or rooster tail it is possible to hang up your boat or spin it around. If the near-the-surface rock is not smooth it could do damage to your craft, especially to inflatables. After the rise, for rocks very near the surface, a *hole* follows—immediately downstream from the rock the

Rock Just Below the Surface

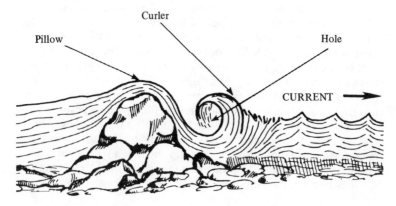

Curler

Pillow

Hole

CURRENT ⟶

water drops sharply forming a depression. Holes and the waves below them are notorious boat eaters. Even the small ones can be a problem if you hit them sideways. Holes also are caused by vertical drops (waterfalls) as well as below the surface rocks. After the drop over a rock, the water comes up from the base of large holes to form a *curler* (or reversal), a wave that curls back upstream. Curlers can flip a boat that is coming up out of the hole. Curlers also add a holding action to a hole—kayakers play in holes, using the upstream part of the curler to hold them in place.

It is very important to spot large holes ahead of time so you can avoid them. Sometimes that's difficult in fast water. If there is any doubt, scout from the bank. Getting alongside (and preferably a little above) a rapid, the frothing, crashing whitewater which follows the pillow is usually very obvious. Scouting from a boat is harder because big holes are the result of big drops—you can't get the perspective necessary to see the whitewater sometimes until just as you start to drop. Look for the smooth pillow. It usually appears as a calm spot, often showing a clearly defined horizontal line in otherwise uneven, ripply water. If you spot what appears to be a pillow, then look for mist rising just beyond it. The mist is the result of the tumbling whitewater in the hole.

Strainers

One of the most formidable obstacles to safe whitewater floating is the strainer. Think of the action of a sieve. A strainer is anything in the river which allows the current to freely pass, but does not give sufficient space for you or your boat. Most common are trees or brush (most dangerous along the outside of turns), but certain configurations of above or just below the surface rocks are also hazardous. A recent lethal entrapment occurred on the Rogue River when a kayaker came out of his boat and his leg became wedged between two rocks about two feet below the surface. The strong current kept his leg pinned and his head underwater. Stay very clear of strainers!

Ledges

Another very serious obstacle to safe floating is created by ledges—symmetrical obstructions below the water's surface. Ledges that are parallel with the river flow are usually not a problem, except if they might hang you up or damage your boat. However, lateral ledges, including dams, are notoriously dangerous. They can form an unavoidable hole, one that extends all the way across the river! Entrapment in a hole is usually solved by moving laterally. That tactic won't

Always remain alert in whitewater, choosing your route carefully.
(Courtesy of Whitewater Manufacturing)

work for holes created by lateral ledges, because either direction you go there is just more hole and more curler preventing downstream progress. Making matters worse, ledges are often very hard to spot from the boat. Look for a sudden quickening of current, a long horizontal line with a mist coming up behind it, or any indication along either shoreline of an abrupt drop. If you don't spot a ledge (even a little one of 2 or 3 feet) and go over it, chances are you'll spend a long time in the foamy water which is moving upstream just below the drop. Someone will probably have to throw you a line from 10 or 20 feet downstream to pull you out. What often happens, the boat capsizes and ultimately washes out of the hole; if it's a slow process in cold water your life may be at risk.

Main Current

Any experienced river runner has learned how to make sense out of the river's varying current speed. Even in flat, calm water, some areas of the river are moving faster than others. Use the main (strongest) current to float you through calm water more quickly, especially when dealing with a headwind. In rapids, the main current about three-quarters of the time is the best route for safe passage. When in doubt, go for fast water. The river tends to run faster in the least obstructed pathway. Also, if you like tailwaves, the large ones always are in strong current. Generally, only when the main current leads into obstacles would a boatman stay out of it.

Classification of Rapids

Reading the river is a critical skill for whitewater floating, essential if you wish to become proficient at running rapids. Dumb luck isn't much to count on when you're encountering big water. Even for runs you have made a dozen times, if the water level or other conditions change, it's like a brand new river and you need to be able to spot trouble before you get into it. All experienced river runners have long since learned the importance of water level to the characteristics of any rapid. As the level goes up or down, a section of whitewater can become markedly less or more tricky, markedly less or more dangerous! Herein lies a problem with guidebooks—they have to represent a certain water level(s) and any significant change from that and you can probably throw them away.

Classifiction of Rapids

Class	Label	Description
I	Practice	Only minor waves and ripples, easy to find course, very minor obstacles.
II	Novice	Minimal maneuvering required, waves three feet or less, no dangerous hazards.
III	Intermediate	Some maneuvering required around rocks and/or holes, waves under five feet, course not always recognizable, consider scouting.
IV	Advanced	Multiple hazards—rocks, large holes, strong cross currents, sharp turns, etc., waves over five feet, should be scouted.
V	Expert	Extremely difficult and complicated series of hazards usually including large drops, very dangerous, must scout.
VI	Unrunnable	Virtually impossible to float safely in ordinary river craft, high likelihood of injury or death.

In order to simply and efficiently describe the difficulty of various rapids, most people in this country use a six-point system of whitewater classification borrowed from Europe called the International Scale. It leaves a lot to be desired in that it creates some argument as to the particular number for a particular rapid depending upon who is doing the rating. The problem is that several factors must be considered simultaneously in applying the rating system (for example, number and depth of drops, height of waves, and number of course changes required). Therefore, one Class III rapid may be a simple seven-foot drop followed by a big tailout, where another Class III might be a trickly little rock garden maze with no holes or drops or waves to speak of. A rater who de-emphasizes drops may give the first kind of rapid a II rating, where someone used to lots of rocky rapids may downgrade the second to a II. Despite the problems inherent in multi-factor rating by less than perfect human beings, the existing system is much better than nothing. It will give you an indication of the difficulty and danger of a rapid, give or take a half-point or so, for the water level at which it was rated. Finally, many people use "+" (for example, II+ or IV+) to handle those rapids which seem to fall in between two of the numbers.

Examples of Rapids

In order to take this discussion of the classification of rapids out of the abstract, given below are brief descriptions for running actual rapids (two for each of the first five classes). From these you should get a sense of how difficult each succeeding number becomes. These descriptions also are related to give novice whitewater boaters some notion as to the kinds of hazards rapids present and what must be done to avoid them (the routes are for all boats, the instructions are for rowing).

Class I: Oak Flats Riffle (Illinois River, Oregon). The approach to this rapid is a clear pool. You must move far left to enter the tongue beginning a clear chute down the left side and float a tailout with 3- to 4-foot waves.

Class I: Clam Beds Riffle (Rogue River, Oregon). As you near this rapid an island is evident in the river ahead. The wide right channel is very shallow and generally impassable. The left channel turns left and heads for a steep, rocky bank. Enter on the right side of the left channel and head for the bank, bow first. The water bouncing off the wall will turn you downstream through a gentle tailout.

Class II: Flat Rock Rapid (North Umpqua, Oregon). As you enter the fast chute, you'll see lots of boulders to the right and to the left. Enter in the exact middle of the 50-foot long chute and immediately assume a ferry position (not too sharply angled because of the waves). At the base of the chute, right square in front of you, is a picnic table-sized boulder. You must increase your ferry angle and slip to the right of it.

Class II: Upper Galice Riffle (Rogue River, Oregon). This rapid starts as another rapid ends, its beginning indicated only by a sharp right turn. Identify a rock centered in midstream and a large hole just past it on the left side of the river. Pass to the left of the guard rock, then pull hard to move to the right of the hole, then take the drop and ride the tailwaves.

Class III: Whistling Bird Rapid (Owyhee River, Oregon). A large rockslab has slid into the river, and along with several boulders, dangerously plugs up the right side. The left side is very shallow and rocky. Enter the rapid mistream, but as far left as possible, brushing rocks with your left sidetube—your course will take you right up to two large boulders just to the left of the giant slab. Pivot left off the cushion in front of the boulders and drop through the hole and waves on the left.

Class III: Lumgrey Creek Rapid (Klamath River, California). You have a choice here. The left channel is an extremely narrow, rocky, fast water chute with a sharp right turn at the bottom. Near the bottom as you hit the turn you'll need to make some adjustments laterally to clear some rocks on the left. The key to the right channel is the entry. You must brush a pyramid-shaped rock on the left at the top and enter the 6-foot drop bow first. Downstream you'll have to work around some boulders on the right. Either channel you choose, chances are better than 90 percent you'll hit some rocks (usually just below the surface)—it's a good rapid to practice 360 degree turns.

Class IV: Blossom Bar Rapid (Rogue River, Oregon). Refer to the elaborate description of this rapid, a delightful technical run, in Chapter V.

Class IV: Rock Dam Rapid (Owyhee River, Oregon). The major difficulty, especially at lower water levels, is the entry—it is virtually impossible in a large raft to enter without scraping near the surface rocks (and getting out of shape for the boulders and holes immediately downstream). The place of entry is the right middle. The left is completely impassable, as it is heavily choked with large boulders. The right side is a concrete diversion channel which is narrow and makes a 90-degree left turn after about 30 feet. After you bump and scrape your way through the entry, pull off of a wrap rock about 20 feet from the top on your left side. Then pull back a little to the left and line up straight to punch through a hole and the waves behind it.

Class V: Hell's Corner Rapid (Klamath River, Oregon). This is a long, narrow, rocky rapid that dumps directly into a class IV drop. Enter just right of a large standing wave at the top and then identify the jagged submerged boulder ahead and pass immediately along its right side. Stay in the chute on the right side of the river, passing through several 4- to 6-foot drops. When the river begins to turn left, keep in the middle of the river to avoid the boulders on your right. As the river swings back to the right, hug the right bank—all the rest of the river to your left is full of boulders. From here you'll drop into another rapid called the Dragon.

Class V: Green Wall Rapid (Illinois River, Oregon). The Green Wall is in a 300-yard long boulder-choked canyon. The first third of the rapid is relatively open and requires staying in midstream, avoiding boulders as necessary. As you finish this part, a solid rock cliff begins on the right and in front of you are four large boulders in a line. You must drop through between the two middle boulders and immediately pull hard right (to pass to the right of a boulder 20 feet in front of you). For the next 60 yards the river drops repeatedly, finishing with the biggest drop of about 10 feet. After that drop you'll have to avoid the tremendous hydraulics coming off the right wall without getting caught by the boulders on the left.

To summarize this chapter, proper evaluation of all potential hazards in a whitewater rapid is a learned skill, one acquired through patience and practice. Anyone can spot a car-sized, above-the-surface rock from the bank, but an expert river runner can forecast trouble from more subtle cues like ripples on the surface of the water or rising mist behind a horizontal line of calm water. He recognizes the ripples as subsurface rocks and the mist as an impeding drop, and can make these judgments with just a glance from a few feet above river level—but no one is born with this ability. Generally, you should always stop to scout any new Class III or Class IV rapid you encounter, and always scout even a familiar Class V or VI (if you run VI's). Standing on the shore alongside a new rapid with a group of expert boatmen discussing a route through rock-infested big whitewater is always a pleasure. A high level of river reading is something to be admired.

—————— # Chapter 5

Rowing Skills

AS STATED EARLIER, THERE ARE TWO ESSENTIAL kinds of learning that must occur to take the luck out of boating. First, you must acquire the ability to read the river, that is recognize and understand the various hydraulics which occur in whitewater rapids. Once this ability is in place it only remains that you have sufficient control of your craft to put it where you know it should be. This chapter describes the basic techniques of whitewater rowing for use by boatmen piloting rafts, catarafts, and drift boats. The next chapter is devoted to paddling, both singly and in groups for paddle rafting.

For any kind of boat, work to achieve maximum control of your craft. For any size of rapid, including the little ones, take pride in precision. If you've run a rapid before try to make today's run even better, rowing or paddling it nearer to perfect than the last time. If the ideal place to be, for example, is one foot to the left of a particular midstream boulder, then work to miss it by exactly one foot. Think about and learn from your mistakes. And above all, don't get lazy. More than a few good boatmen have tempted disaster because they let overconfidence make them sloppy. For many, the third or fourth run through a major rapid is their worst, even though their ability to read water and boating skills were better than on earlier trips. And finally, if you get out of shape, keep working and don't give up. If you stay on the oars you often can pull yourself out of terrible situations.

Basic Techniques

As you sit at the oars, there are really only three maneuvers you can make with a raft: Turning (right or left), rowing forward, or rowing backward (flipping upside down is not included since it is generally unplanned and undesirable). The last one, rowing backward, is by far the most important.

Rowing Backward

If the bow of your boat is facing downstream, by reaching forward with the oar handles and then pulling, you effectively are rowing backward and upstream, moving in the opposite direction of the current. Unless the water speed is extremely slow, you won't really make progress backwards that would literally take you upstream. Instead, rowing backwards with your raft oriented parallel to the river flow just serves to slow down your forward movement—your raft won't move downstream as fast as the current. And rowing backward is an extremely strong stroke. You can lean forward and involve most of your body to pull back hard on the oars.

In reality, rowers almost constantly row backwards in big rapids, but rarely do so with their boat pointed directly downstream. It is helpful to pull on the oars to slow the boat, but even more important to be able to move laterally across the river to avoid obstacles. By turning your boat, anywhere from 10 to 80 degrees, you can accomplish both at the same time—you will both slow the boat and move away from whatever is beyond the bow. Hence, the whitewater rower's number one guideline: Point at what you don't want to hit!

Back Ferry

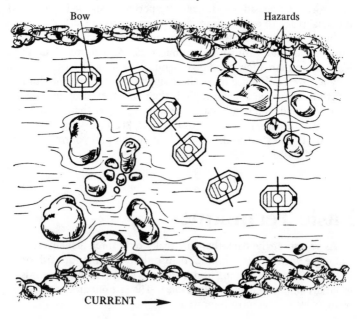

CURRENT →

Angled back rowing is known as *back ferrying*. It is the standard technique used for maneuvering rafts away from hazards in whitewater. The angle should be adjusted depending on the speed of the current and how rapidly you need to effect lateral movement. Although it can be dangerous in an area of waves and holes (you may flip the raft), sometimes the only means to avoiding a serious hazard directly in front of you is to turn your boat almost completely sideways and pull hard and fast. In most conditions you can avoid severe ferry angles by properly reading the river and anticipating the hazards.

Blossom Bar Rapids

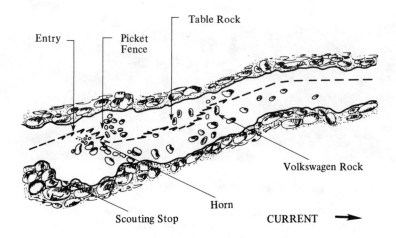

A good example rapid to elaborate the use of the back ferry in big water is Blossom Bar Rapid on the Rogue River in southern Oregon. Blossom is a 400-foot long rock garden with a noticeable drop near the top. At typical summer water levels the only entry to the rapids is on the left, about 10 feet from a sheer rock wall. The right side is so full of large boulders that it is virtually impassable. You enter into medium speed whitewater which rapidly picks up velocity and slams into a row of closely spaced rocks directly in front of you. Those rocks collectively are known as the "Picket Fence" and you need to move right to avoid them. It is estimated that this hazard destroys dozens of drift boats each year and uncounted numbers of rafts and smaller paddled boats flip or wrap. When you enter Blossom Bar Rapid, do so as far right in that left channel as is safe. Immediately point your bow toward the left wall (at an angle of 20 to 30 degrees). To get some momentum and rhythm going, start

Floater's view when approaching the Picket Fence in Blossom Bar Rapid.

taking gentle pulls on the oars as soon as you get into the ferry position. As you get closer to the Picket Fence you'll pull harder and harder while simultaneously increasing the severity of your ferry angle. Then, only 20 feet or so from disaster, take four or five massive strokes and you'll catch an eddy on the downstream side of a large rock just above the drop (called the "Horn"). Done correctly, you've moved out of that left channel which heads into the Picket Fence and are now almost exactly midstream. Everything seems slow motion above the drop as you maintain about a 45-degree ferry angle with the bow pointed left. Stroke gently to assure that you clear the far right rock of the Picket Fence—you are pointed at what you don't want to hit. When you are sure you will be clear, pull the right oar to swing your bow straight downstream and take the drop. As you get into the waves after the drop, point the front of your boat a little to the right and take a few strokes—there's an unnamed boulder that you might brush downstream 40 feet or so. Ferrying here can be tricky because it is sometimes hard to get a good pull in up and down, frothy waves.

Once you avoid the Picket Fence and successfully travel through the Horn, the rapid becomes a little easier to run. However, there are still two more critical lateral moves you will need to make. In front of you and to the left is Table Rock, a large flat-topped boulder with a hole behind it. Point your bow toward it and pull away gently so that you just barely clear the right side of it. Now, nearly dead ahead is Volkswagen Rock (shaped like a VW Beetle). As you clear Table Rock assume a severe ferry angle, bow pointed toward the right shore. Pull hard and you'll go to the left of Volkswagen Rock—there are also some small rocks on the left to avoid during this pull. Once you clear this last major obstacle, the water speed and difficulty both drop for the remainder of the rapid. Ferry to the right around the boulder directly in your path and then just pick your way on through.

Large raft approaching the Horn, the tongue ahead and to the boatman's left, in Blossom Bar Rapid.

A lot of river runners dichotomize whitewater runs into "big water" and "technical water." Big water rivers are like the Colorado River in Arizona and the Main Salmon in Idaho. These rivers are characterized by a large volume of water flow, and by massive waves. Once into rapids in these rivers you are pretty much unable to move laterally— just try to keep your boat pointed straight ahead. The phrase "technical water" usually indicates that the river is choked with narrow canyons and lots of boulders (like the Rogue River or the Chatooga from the movie "Deliverance"). You will be required to make a lot of course changes. As you learn to back ferry, find easy rapids with occasional rocks to work your way around. Practice turning your boat and pulling away from them.

Rowing Forward

Rowing forward is accomplished by bringing the oar handles up to your chest and then pushing. This stroke is not as strong as pulling since it is done mostly with your arms. Rowing forward is used only rarely in big whitewater rapids, not only because it is a weaker stroke, but because it speeds your raft up (which gives you less time to move away from obstacles). Occasionally, to get through an unavoidable hole or to escape an eddy or to get over rocks just under the surface a boatman may push the oars for the increased speed. In very mild whitewater you can use forward rowing to maneuver laterally—point in the direction you want to move and push—this is called the *forward ferry*. For most boatmen, the major use of forward rowing is to speed up progress through sections of calm flatwater between rapids and use a different set of muscles to do so.

Turning

Turning is accomplished primarily by stroking one oar, usually by pulling it (again because of the strength of the stroke). You also can push it or just dip it in the current lightly, a stroke used most often to keep the bow straight ahead in fast water and waves. Pulling on the right oar will point the bow at the right shore, and vice versa. You can spot a novice oarsman because often under any pressure at all you will see them turn the wrong way. The wrong way turn is usu-ally followed by a massive overcorrection, sometimes to the point of spinning their boat around backwards. Even harder than learning what oar to pull is learning how hard to pull it—depending upon the water speed, nearness of hazards, and so on, pulls to turn rafts vary from gentle and brief to extremely strong. If you are just beginning,

Rowing: Six Turning Strokes

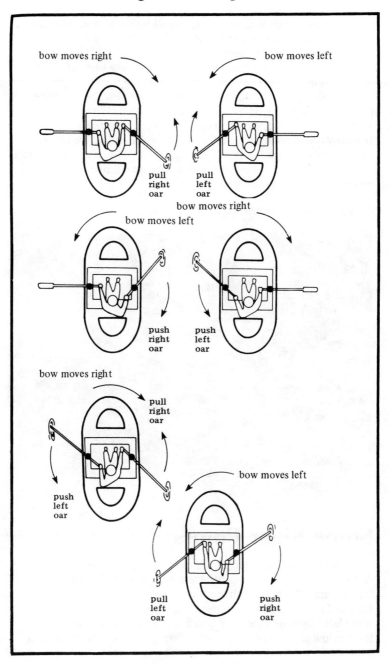

be patient; with practice, which oar to pull (or push or dip) to move either direction and how hard to stroke becomes second nature, almost like the oars are extensions of your arms.

There are occasional times when you must make very rapid turns, or have to turn against currents coming from the side of your craft. In fast water, catarafts tend to resist movement into a ferry position (because both pontoons are working at odds with the river current when you try to turn them). You can make more rapid, stronger turns, by simultaneously pushing one oar while pulling the other. *Double oar turns* are fun to practice in flat water—you can turn your boat into a merry-go-round. Sooner or later you'll find yourself spun around backwards in fast water, and that practice will pay off.

Oars in position to execute a double oar turn.

Some Finer Points

Thus far in this chapter, the basics of rowing have been covered. A boatman needs to be comfortable with rowing backward and rowing forward, and doing both kinds of rowing parallel to the river flow and at various ferrying angles. To accomplish a ferry, that is, to move laterally across the river, you have to learn how to turn. Related below are a series of tips, some finer points for the whitewater rafter.

Bow Straight Ahead

A lot of the work facing a boatman in whitewater rapids is conceptually very simple—keep the bow straight ahead. Sometimes there are hydraulics working against you, sometimes people get lazy. Float through whitewater with your oars poised a foot or two above the surface of the water, and dip them as necessary. When you get in big waves, try to hit them dead center, and don't let your boat swing sideways. If you have to run a hole, again hit it straight on, and be prepared to make instant corrections if the turbulent water tosses you around. Holes and waves are boat flippers if you are not properly oriented. A ten-man raft is about 14 feet long, plenty long enough to ride through all but the largest of waves and holes. But hit it sideways and now as far as the river is concerned you're sitting in a six and one-half foot long boat! If you cannot avoid hitting a rock or steep bank, try to hit it head on with the bow. If you don't, you may end up flipped, swamped or wrapped.

Cataraft preparing to float through a hole, bow straight-ahead.

In whitewater, the majority of your strokes to keep your bow straight ahead should be quick and shallow. This will prevent over-correction and minimize the chance of banging the blades on rocks below the surface. Always be alert to where your blades are dipping. As described earlier, I once got out of sorts in a Class IV rapid and dipped my right oar too deep among a bunch of rocks. The blade caught and the oar flipped out of my hand and into the river. This lack of attention to the water I was rowing in put me in the precarious position of finishing the rapid, including a horrendous hole and 6-foot high tailwaves, with only one oar. I know from experience now, it is possible to keep your bow straight ahead by pulling and pushing only one oar.

Possible Obstacles

The notion presented in this section is taken from the old adage "better safe than sorry." There may be a large number of obstacles in a whitewater rapid that pose no problem because they are on either side of your route. However, in big rapids the river can surprise you and move you laterally depending on the operating currents. If you spot hazards that "maybe" will brush your boat, don't wait until you hit them to find out how close you are going to get. Unless he needs his bow straight ahead for the moment because of a hole or wave, an experienced boatman angles slightly to the side with a possible obstacle—if it begins to change from possibility to reality, he is already prepared to pull away from it.

A common place to see the possible obstacle rule in action is in bends in the river. When going around a bend it is smart to keep angled a little, with your bow pointed at the outside of the turn. If the river current forces you too near the bank, you are all set to pull away. This rule can be especially important when trees and brush overhang the water from that outside bank.

Planning ahead is a sign of a good boatman. Use the river as much as possible, instead of your oars. Beginners battle the currents, experts use them. If a ferry is necessary to avoid an obstacle, don't wait until you're on top the hazard to begin turning and backward rowing. Get some momentum going in your favor way ahead of time if possible. As soon as you clear it, then immediately position your boat to miss the next one. If you get into a situation where hitting a rock is unavoidable, have a plan; like bumping bow first, then spinning off it to the right, then a double oar turn as soon as possible to complete a 360-degree pivot. A good boatman is always thinking ahead, not just reacting.

Shipping Oars

There are some occasions, especially in smaller rivers, where you have no choice but to float right alongside of large boulders or steep canyon walls. When there is rock alongside your boat instead of river you will need to ship an oar, that is, get them out of the water and out of the way. In some narrow chutes or canyons you will have to ship both oars. It is possible to ship oars with the blades forward or the blades backward. Best for momentary shipping, lean well forward and bring the blades backwards. If you choose to ship the oars with the blades forward and atop the raft tubes, bring the handles back behind you—if you ship this direction, be extremely careful to keep the blades from hitting anything outside the boat. I have heard stories of blades not quite in the raft ramming rocks and driving the handle with great force into the boatman's stomach or leg. If I ship the blades forward I ask my passengers to hold them. For those of you using open oarlocks, if you only need a couple of feet, you can pull an oar laterally into the boat.

Passenger is holding the oar blades to keep them shipped in a fast, narrow channel.

Whenever your boat is moving, never allow the oars to dangle freely in the river. An experienced boatman and friend once just about went upside down in a "frog water" drift when an untended oar blade jammed a surprise rock below the surface. Even if tipping is not a possibility, you'll increase your oar life by avoiding banging and bumping the blades. If you don't want to have to hold the oars, ship them by pulling the handles over to the opposite tubes or by just hooking the handles under the bend behind your knees.

Weight Distribution

Inflatable rafts are remarkably forgiving. They bend and flex with the hydraulics of the river, almost without regard for how heavily they are loaded or how the weight is distributed. An important rule of boating is don't overload your craft. If you do, it will become sluggish and slow to respond to the oars. If you take on much water, bail it out as soon as possible. Water is remarkably heavy. The weight you carry should be fairly evenly distributed. The raft (and especially the drift boat) should not be lop-sided in any direction as it floats down the river. On extended trips with lots of gear, avoid the natural inclination to overload the storage area behind the rower. If you bury the stern deep in the water, rowing backward (the most important whitewater rafting stroke) will become noticeably more difficult. When you try to slow up, to back ferry, your craft will not be responsive.

The weight in the boat from the boatman and passengers can be shifted in case of emergency. If the boat begins tipping sideways, through a hole or on the edge of a wave or up against a rock, try to shift your weight to the high side. Be sure to inform your passengers of this principle at the onset of the trip. On several occasions I have seen wraps avoided because everybody in the boat scrambled up on top of the high side tube as a raft washed sideways up against a boulder. The weight shift allows the low side to come up and the river to flow under it—the raft then slides down off the rock and is level again. On one occasion I had to take some weight out of the boat to ensure safe passage through an extremely rocky rapid. The water level was very low and boats were hanging up and spinning around, putting them in serious jeopardy of a wrap on some of the large above-the-surface boulders. I unloaded the passengers and some gear and ran the whitewater alone, 500 pounds lighter.

Lining and Portage

There are occasions, like the rocky rapid described above, where you should consider not running. If you don't run a rapid you have

two options: Let the boat float it without you (lining) or carry the
boat and everything in it down the shoreline until you get past the
whitewater (portage).

Lining a boat can sometimes be tricky. The principle is that by
attaching long ropes to your raft, you can control its course through
a rapid and then pull it over to shore when it reaches calm water.
However, hanging on to a rope tied to a loaded raft in fast whitewater
can be like grabbing a tiger by the tail. A commercial guide died recently on the Rogue River—he was standing on the bank holding
on to a rope.

Lining a raft through a boulder-strewn section of whitewater.
(Courtesy of Whitewater Manufacturing).

Floating Whitewater Rivers

Always line only one boat at a time. Generally, one rope is tied to the bow and one to the stern, with one or more persons holding on to each rope. Try to keep the boat as close as possible to the bank. If it is forced out toward midstream, pull it back in near shore as soon as possible. If the water is shallow, some help may be added by people wading in and pushing and pulling the boat around and over rocks. Those holding the ropes should take special care not to get their fingers, hands, arms or legs tangled in loose rope. Do not tie any ropes to anybody. And everybody involved should be wearing life jackets!

If lining sounds laborious, it doesn't hold a candle to some of the portages I've seen. Taking your boat and all its gear down the shoreline for many rivers means up and over and around boulders, trees, brush and steep banks. If you have a lot of people and not much gear, just surround your boat and pick it up. If the going is tough or you have a large amount of gear or very few people, take all the gear downstream first. Then, come back and get the raft. If you are scrambling through thick trees and brush, you should consider deflating the boat. Deflated and wrapped around your oars, it is a fairly manageable package for two people. Portaging drift boats can be even more difficult than moving rafts. Some of the wood ones are very heavy, and no matter what they're made of, you can't fold them or reduce their bulk. Often, rather than lift and carry them, people tie ropes to the bow and literally drag them around a rapid.

—————— # Chapter 6

Paddling Skills

THIS CHAPTER WILL BE DEVOTED TO THOSE WHO PRE-
fer to paddle, either solo as in most kayaks, or in groups as for
paddle rafting. Generally speaking, the techniques are the same for
all paddlers. The differences that do exist will be elaborated upon
below. Presuming you have the right length paddle (see Chapter II
for single blade and Chapter III for double blade paddles), check
your grip. If you hang on to the shaft with both hands and set the
paddle on your head, both forearms should be at right angles to the
shaft. You will lose a lot of leverage and power if your hands are too
close together. Also, for double-bladed paddles, your hands should
be equidistant from the blades.

Basic Techniques

Where backward rowing was the oarsman's fundamental stroke,
forward paddling is the basic stroke for paddlers. It is the easiest to
learn and physically the strongest. Also important skills to learn are
backward paddling, drawing and bracing.

Paddling Forward

For nearly straight ahead locomotion, paddle as follows. Put the
paddle blade in the water as far forward as you can comfortably reach.
Pull the blade through the water toward the stern, keeping it close to
the boat during the entire stroke. By rotating your torso you can get
the maximum length out of this stroke—the shoulder on the side on
which you are paddling is first pushed forward, and then pulled back.
Allow your upper body to be relaxed and flexible, so you can rotate
comfortably from the waist up as you stroke. As you do all this,
make sure the blade's face is oriented for maximum power as it moves
through the water, then turned slightly to knife its way out when the
stroke is completed. Forward paddling propels your craft forward
and slightly turns it (away from the stroke side). If you wish to gain
more turning action from the stroke, instead of keeping the blade near

Kayaker forward-paddling upstream, ferrying to move laterally across the river.

the boat, allow it to *sweep* a large half-circle from bow to stern. Sweeping will decrease the forward motion it gives your boat proportionate to the distance the blade is away from mid-ship. The wider the half-circle, the more the boat will turn.

It is rare to see paddle rafters do anything but close-to-the boat forward paddling. Since there are usually the same number of paddlers on both sides of the raft, the stroke does not produce any perceptible turn. The same is true for two-paddler canoes, once the two boatmen learn to work together. Relatively straight progress in the small solo boats is accomplished by alternating sides as you paddle. Kayakers often turn their boats upstream, angle slightly, then paddle straight ahead alternating sides, keeping the blades close to the boat. This is *forward ferrying* and it slows their boats (relative to the current) while moving them laterally across the river away from hazards. It is important that as you increase the angle of your ferry in a small boat, you lean downstream to prevent water from flowing over the top of your craft and capsizing it.

Paddling Backward

Paddlers can also stroke from stern to bow, to slow themselves in the current (when facing downstream) or back ferry to move perpendicular to the river flow. For this stroke it is very important to keep the blade very close to the boat to avoid radically turning small craft. If you wish turning action simultaneously, allow the blade to sweep a semi-circular arc alongside your boat. This is very useful when a strong, swift maneuver is needed to avoid a hazard—it will turn your boat's bow toward the stroke side and slow your forward progress. This procedure is usually followed by back ferrying away from the obstacle (again leaning downstream in smaller craft). For maximum power, whether stroking parallel to the boat or sweeping, rotate your torso as you paddle.

Paddler closing in to help another river runner.

Paddling: Four Turning Strokes

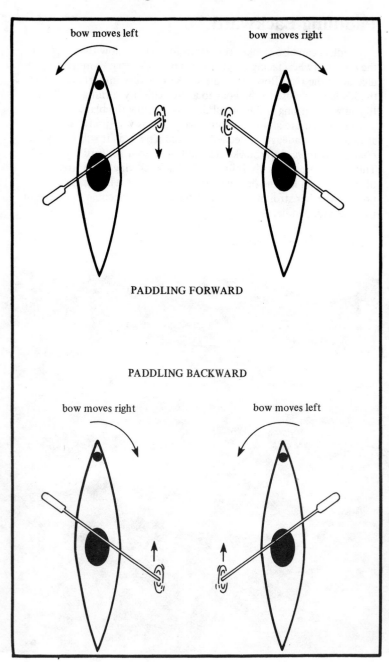

bow moves left

bow moves right

PADDLING FORWARD

PADDLING BACKWARD

bow moves right

bow moves left

Drawing

As can be seen from the preceding discussions, forward and backward paddling as a means to turning always simultaneously has some effect on forward motion. The draw stroke is accomplished by reaching out sideways with the blade face parallel with your boat, then pulling straight toward the side of your boat. If you draw stroke to the middle of your craft, the entire boat will move to the side of the stroke—I have seen novice kayakers move all the way across a swimming pool this way. It's a little smoother getting your blade out of the water if you turn it perpendicular to the boat before lifting it. To turn with very little effect on forward motion, you can execute the draw stroke by leaning forward and pulling the blade up to the bow of your boat. A *bow draw* pulls the nose of the craft toward the side of the stroke.

Bracing

The previously discussed strokes are all basic to moving to where you want to be in the river. Bracing is a stroke with a different purpose—to keep your boat upright. Small craft tend to be "tippy," especially in heavy currents and waves. In a brace stroke you are literally stroking from the surface of the water downward. To practice a simple brace stroke, lean to one side, as if a wave from the other side was pushing you over. Then slap the water with the face of the blade of your paddle on the side to which you leaned. This will push you back upright. If you are going to practice bracing in

Kayaker completing a roll to upright a capsized boat.

a hard-shell kayak, have a friend assist you. It is very common to capsize when first leaning the stroke and he can flip you back over.

An even more effective uprighting maneuver is the *sweeping brace*. The paddle blade orientation is critical here. Split the difference between flat and perpendicular, between a simple brace and a simple sweep. With the blade at about a 45-degree angle and using your whole upper body, lean to one side and sweep brace that side. Done properly, the blade face will plane across the top of the water throughout the stroke.

A common injury to kayakers, and one that comes from sweeping braces, is shoulder dislocation. Keep the elbow of your upper arm in tight and as close as possible to your chest. Don't allow that arm to be extended above your head. There are a couple of tricks some kayakers use to increase their leverage when sweep bracing. The upper hand may be slipped upward until it touches the blade. Not only is there some mechanical advantage to this, but you can literally feel the orientation of your blade (helpful in roily water that is bouncing you all over). Some paddlers, for the same reasons as slipping the hand up the shaft, grab the upper blade of their paddle with their upper arm hand.

A maneuver that is specific to hard-shell kayaks is the *roll*. The only option to learning how to roll your boat back upright whenever you capsize (which can be often in big rapids) is to bail completely out of it—something all kayakers should practice, just in case. It is very unlikely with you hanging upside down in the water beneath your kayak like a giant keel that it will right itself. The roll is essentially nothing more than a sweeping brace. From upside down, lean to one side and sweep from bow to stern, making sure that the face of the blade starts on the surface of the water and planes across the top of it. Blade orientation is critical—you want your blade to "pull" on the water, not knife through it. My description may make rolling sound easy, but the initial disorientation at being upside down as you are learning usually makes it difficult. However, if you have previously mastered the sweeping brace from an upright position, can get a friend to help you, and are willing to practice, rolling can be as easy as tying your shoes (almost). Be aware that rolling in heavy whitewater is significantly more difficult than doing it in a swimming pool or other calm water. Work hard to get very proficient at it in flat water before you need it in a rapid. The fine tuning for kayakers only begins with the roll. Beyond this skill there are many other refinements, and with further work, soon you will be doing 180-degree turns into eddies then "peeling off" them, surfing on waves, doing pop-ups and endos, and so on.

Some Finer Points

Related thus far in this chapter are the basic strokes paddlers use to negotiate whitewater rivers. Much of the discussion under "Some Finer Points" for oared boats (Chapter V) applies here, with some important differences and additions discussed below. Also, paddle rafting adds some dimensions to solo paddling that will be elaborated upon.

Paddle Rafting

The majority of paddle rafters I've encountered are part of "do-it-yourself" commercial trips. It is all the lead paddler (the person on the stern, employed by the outfitter) can do to get his group of novices to forward paddle straight ahead on his command. However, a paddle raft operated by a well-practiced, strong team of whitewater experts is a pleasure to watch. Generally, one person is selected as the captain—he makes all the decisions, issues aloud all the commands, and sits on the stern using his paddle blade like a rudder to

Paddle rafting requires precision teamwork. (Courtesy of Whitewater Manufacturing)

Paddle Rafting: Six Turning Strokes

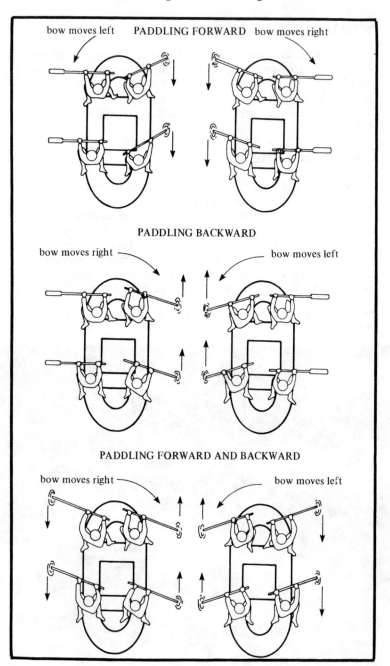

bow moves left   PADDLING FORWARD   bow moves right

PADDLING BACKWARD

bow moves right   bow moves left

PADDLING FORWARD AND BACKWARD

bow moves right   bow moves left

keep the boat straight or to control turns. Before beginning, it is important to make certain that there is fairly even power on both sides of the boat and that all paddlers are well braced. This is usually accomplished by hooking toes under a thwart—never tie anybody into a boat! There are available non-entrapping foot braces that can be glued into your raft. In rocking and rolling big rapids it is not unusual to see one or more paddlers who didn't properly brace flipped into the water. Without a frame the raft is much less rigid, tending to roll and buck more with the waves and turbulence, but also tending to have more resistance to capsizing.

With a group of paddlers in a raft there are two basic strokes, forward and backward. If all boatmen forward stroke the boat goes straight ahead. When this is done at an angle, facing upstream, it is forward ferrying as described earlier (the most powerful ferry for paddled craft). If all boatmen backward paddle, facing downstream, the raft is slowed in the current; if the boat is angled, then the craft is back ferrying. The most common approach to turning is simply to command only one side to forward paddle and the raft will turn to the non-paddling side. If you have only one side backward paddle, the boat's bow will swing to the paddling side as well as slowing up a little. For the most rapid and powerful turn, one side can forward paddle while the other strokes backward (the same principle as the double-oar turn for rowing).

While turning, the person on the stern needs only to angle his blade out to the side in the direction of the desired turn. To speed up a turn, rather than simply ruddering, the stern paddler can reach out and make a draw stroke. Finally, very well-trained paddle raft crews can properly execute the "draw and pry" technique to move sideways in the river. While on one side all paddlers are making draw strokes, the other side is prying. To *pry* stroke, put your blade in the water so that it is lying flat against the raft tube and your upper arm is out over the water. By pushing with your lower arm at the same time you pull your upper arm in, you effectively are making a stroke sideways from the boat, creating the exact opposite effect of drawing.

Other Tips

For all sizes of paddled craft, most of the finer points from the chapter on rowing hold true. With inflatable boats, be especially alert to the bow straight ahead and weight distribution guidelines. Probably the only major difference in these finer points for rowing as compared to paddling is that paddled craft often do not "point at what they don't want to hit." Instead, paddlers generally point in exactly the opposite direction so they can rely upon their strongest stroke, paddling forward, to stay out of trouble. Thus, you will see kayaks going around a bend in the river facing the inside of the turn (and slightly upstream). I once saw several rafts float a long, rocky, fast bend, some paddled and some rowed—at first glance, with them facing in opposite directions, it looked like somebody was terribly confused! For moving laterally, and simultaneously slowing the boat, paddled craft often turn completely around, almost facing upstream, and then forward row. The only real disadvantages to the forward ferry are that it requires a second or two to turn around and that it is harder to see downstream. You need to keep enough angle that you can comfortably swing your head around to look on down the rapid. In small craft, always remember to lean a little downstream so the river current hits the bottom and side of your boat and not the top.

Forward Ferry

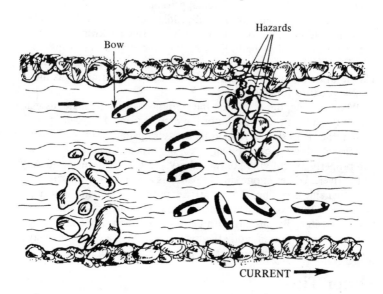

Small boats should regularly utilize eddies for rest and scout breaks, even in the middle of big whitewater. In smaller craft, you sit lower and often are headed sideways or upstream, both making clear views of the obstacles ahead much more difficult. Turning into an eddy gives you a chance to come almost to a complete stop, survey the scene, and plan your next series of moves. Kayakers have developed a special stroke, called the *Duffek*, just for turning into eddies. Facing downstream, begin by sweeping the opposite side to start a turn, heading bow first toward the eddy. Then reach into the eddy water (the water that is very slow or moving upstream) on the other side as if to make a bow draw stroke with one important difference—the face of the blade should be past parallel with the side of your boat, angled a little forward. Pull as in a draw and your kayak will do a 180-degree turn into the eddy, leaving you facing upstream.

Finally, if you are beginner at paddling, and especially if you are a novice solo boatman, learn techniques in calm water. Flat water without current, like a lake or pond, is best. The various strokes presented in this chapter double or triple in difficulty of smooth execution when in roily whitewater. Practice in a place where you don't have constantly changing hydraulics to deal with. Once you think you have got your paddling skills down, then move to easy whitewater and begin practicing in current. Move up through bigger water only as you gain in skill and confidence.

Kayaker holding in an eddy, keeping a watchful eye on a capsized companion.

Chapter 7 _____

River Camping

MOST WHITEWATER ENTHUSIASTS BEGIN RIVER RUN-
ning by short trips on easy water. Through numerous day
and half-day runs they gain experience and get comfortable in what is
at first a novel environment. If you stick with the activity, sooner or
later you'll begin setting up float trips on rivers in places where you
can't drive home at night. Multi-day floats add immensely to the
total experience, to a feeling of connectedness with the river and the
environment through which it flows. Most overnight floats occur in
wilderness or near-wilderness areas, in places where the floaters can
enjoy a part of the world much different from their typically urban
existence. And the sense of camaraderie and togetherness among a
group of people increases ten-fold when a trip spans days rather than
hours. There is time spent sitting around the campfire, sharing meals,
taking hikes, and so on, to bring people closer. In order to reap the
benefits of multi-day floating, however, there is a price to be paid.
For a day trip nearby it takes me about 30 minutes to get ready—I
need boat, oars, ammo boxes, pump, bail bucket, life jacket, a cooler
full of cold drinks and a few other odds and ends. For an extended
wilderness float, it sometimes takes weeks to get it all organized.

General Logistics

The first order of business in planning is to choose a river, then
the particular stretch of that river you want to float. Bear in mind
that many of the best multi-day floats occur on controlled rivers.
You may need *permits*. For example, if you want to float the lower
Rogue River in Oregon (typically a three or four day trip) during the
summer months, you will have to apply to the local office of the
U. S. Forest Service way back in February to have your name entered
into a lottery for permits. You will have to specify the number of
people in your party and the day you wish to set-in. If you don't
get your permits this way (the odds are against you, about four-to-
one), there are provisions for obtaining them from spots created by
cancellations and no-shows.

Once you choose the float you want, check to see if you need permits, and if you do, find out how to obtain them. As part of this process, put together your group: Determine both how many boats and how many people. Generally, a float is more fun and much safer if you gather some people to go with you. Only the most expert and most healthy should consider an extended wilderness solo float, and do so knowing that they have sacrificed some hedge on safety.

When you've gotten to this point in your planning, you'll have to give some thought to the *shuttle*. There needs to be at least one vehicle at the take-out, more as your group gets larger. For some floats, if you intend to do your own shuttle, you'll have to plan an extra day just for the driving. Whenever possible, I prefer to pay local people to do the shuttle for me. On one occasion, for an Owyhee River float in southeastern Oregon, I not only paid for someone to drive a truck and a big station wagon to the take-out, but hired a powerboat to meet us where the Owyhee River dumps into Owyhee Lake for a water shuttle. They towed us across 12 miles of flatwater. I had been warned that when the wind comes up, it can take 8 to 10 hours of heavy pulling to row across the lake. Giving forethought to the logistics of put-in and take-out can save a lot of hassles when the time of the trip arrives. As part of your attention to vehicles, plan ahead for transportation to and from the river; that is, determine who will ride with whom, who carries what boats, when people will arrive, and so on. Don't leave anything to chance!

Next in your plans should be a careful look at the float itself. By talking with people who have run the river before you and obtaining any guidebooks available, sketch out a tentative itinerary. Figure out approximately how many miles you intend to float each day in order to bring your trip to its completion on time. If possible, have particular campsites selected (or at least the general area for stopping each day) before you ever get on the river. Also, learn features to watch for, like stretches of difficult whitewater, mandatory portage points, bits of history (cabins, bridges, mines, and so on), characteristic wildlife and plantlife, and scenic features (rock formations, waterfalls, hot springs, and so on).

Finally, as part of your advance preparation consider gear and meals. For example, if there are six boats, it is not necessary for each to bring a large two-burner stove (presuming you are going to share meals). Various camping items like tents, first-aid kits, stoves, cooking utensils, portable latrines, and so on, can be shared—work that out well in advance. Regarding meals, I like the system where each boat carries and serves its own lunches. Breakfasts and dinners are in-camp, full-group affairs. Depending on the number of boats and people, I assign small subgroups to take care of particular meals (the planning, transporting, preparation, and clean-up). That way, for some meals all you have to do is show up—it's somebody else's turn to cook!

RIVER TRIP CHECKLIST

Boat/Accessories
- ☐ Raft
- ☐ Ethafoam
- ☐ Frame
- ☐ Frame Straps
- ☐ River Bags
- ☐ Bilge Pump
- ☐ Bail Bucket
- ☐ 100-ft. Rope
- ☐ Lashing Rope
- ☐ Stretch Cords
- ☐ Ammo Cans
- ☐ Pump
- ☐ Oars
- ☐ Life Jackets
- ☐ Camera Bag
- ☐ _____
- ☐ _____
- ☐ _____

Repair Items
- ☐ Knife
- ☐ Spare D-Ring
- ☐ Spare Valve
- ☐ Patch Kit
- ☐ Duct Tape
- ☐ Pliers
- ☐ Spare Straps
- ☐ Sandpaper
- ☐ Rag
- ☐ Hardware
- ☐ Thread/Needles
- ☐ _____
- ☐ _____
- ☐ _____
- ☐ _____

Health Care Items
- ☐ Emergency Kit
- ☐ Soap
- ☐ Comb
- ☐ Sunscreen
- ☐ Toothbrush/paste
- ☐ Towel/washcloth
- ☐ Sunglasses
- ☐ Extra Glasses
- ☐ Toilet Paper
- ☐ Insect Repellent
- ☐ _____
- ☐ _____
- ☐ _____

Camping/Cooking
- ☐ Stove
- ☐ Lantern
- ☐ Fuel
- ☐ Flashlight
- ☐ Tent
- ☐ Coolers
- ☐ Ice
- ☐ Sleeping Bags
- ☐ Sleeping Pads
- ☐ Pots/Pans
- ☐ Knives/Forks/ Spoons
- ☐ Coffee Pot
- ☐ Utensils
- ☐ Bowls/Plates/Cups
- ☐ Trash Bags
- ☐ Can Opener
- ☐ Matches
- ☐ Camera
- ☐ Film

Books/Maps
- ☐ _____
- ☐ _____
- ☐ _____

Clothing
RIVER
- ☐ Hat
- ☐ T-shirts
- ☐ Shorts
- ☐ Sneakers
- ☐ Long Pants
- ☐ Wet Suit
- ☐ Wind Top
- ☐ _____
- ☐ _____
- ☐ _____

CAMP
- ☐ Pants
- ☐ Shirts
- ☐ Coat
- ☐ Shoes/Boots
- ☐ Socks
- ☐ Belt
- ☐ Underwear
- ☐ _____
- ☐ _____
- ☐ _____

RAIN
- ☐ Hat
- ☐ Jacket
- ☐ Pants
- ☐ _____

Miscellaneous Items
- ☐ _____
- ☐ _____

As the time nears for your trip, for several days you may feel overwhelmed. There are so many fine details, things not to forget, that it can become a nightmare. After my first few multi-day trips and once having to drive an extra two hours because I forgot my oars, I developed a checklist that I use for all overnight river trips. This one is for rafters—if you are floating a small boat and have no raft support, your list will be a whole lot shorter. Feel free to copy mine if you like, but take the time to customize it to fit your size boat, your needs, your equipment, and your gear. I have to modify it for each trip, crossing out some items I won't need (like raingear in August on a desert river) and add some in the spaces provided (like a firepan when we intend to have a campfire). Remember, as you put together your river trip checklist, you are going to have to carry all those items on your boat—don't overload with so much weight that your craft becomes unresponsive in fast water. As a general rule, the more difficult the river, the more carefully you should select, limit and stow your gear and supplies. Looking at the checklist, the boat and its accessories have been discussed earlier in this book. The Repair Items and Health Care necessities will be considered in Chapter IX, Common Sense and Safety. Prior to talking about camping gear and clothing, we will look at containers designed to keep everything dry and how to load them into your boat.

Waterproof Containers

Basically, you can divide all waterproof containers into two kinds—rigid and non-rigid. As a general rule the rigid containers are smaller, more expensive per volume of storage provided, heavier, and provide the best protection for your most valuable and fragile items (like cameras, lenses, eyeglasses, binoculars, and so on). The most popular rigid containers have always been military surplus *ammunition cans.* They are made of steel and virtually indestructible under normal river running use. They are available in a variety of sizes, some large enough to carry your whole kitchen. Ammo cans have a securely locking lid with a rubber gasket inside. I fished one out of a riffle one time that looked like it had been there for years. I pried the rusty lid off to find the contents entirely dry. You do need to attend to the paint on your ammo cans; they are made of steel and subject to rust if you're not careful. Finally, most of them have substantial handles, important for carrying the larger ones and useful in all sizes for tie-on points when lashing your gear into your boat.

Available commercially are plastic or fiberglass or aluminum waterproof boxes, generally small to medium in size and utilizing a rubber gasket to assure a tight seal. Many large watertight containers are marketed under the name "dry boxes" (most often made of aluminum). Some of the fanciest raft frames employ a large dry box for the passenger seat. For a low-cost rigid container, look into cannisters for bulk food (at restaurants, bakeries, nursing homes or schools). Some of them are remarkably watertight. The achille's heel for any of these various rigid containers is the lid. If you have any doubts, before you entrust your camera or other valuables to one, fill it with water and turn it upside down. The logic here is that if it keeps water in during this test, it will keep water out when you use it on the river. Also, make certain your container has ample, strong tie-on points, and handles if it is large.

Most river runners use *waterproof bags* to carry all their soft gear, like clothes, boots, sleeping bag, tent, and so on. I also use waterproof bags to carry most of the hard gear too, like camp stove, lantern, kitchen equipment and toilet items—anything that needs to be kept dry, but is not likely to break or be otherwise destroyed by a

Assortment of both rigid and non-rigid waterproof containers.

little bouncing around. There are a wide variety of waterproof bags on the market. Generally, the ones made of unbacked vinyl or plastic are not durable or dependable. The best bags are made from the same kinds of materials used to construct rafts (see Chapter II). Even then don't trust the label "watertight" without testing it in the same way described for rigid waterproof containers. Bags come in a variety of sizes and shapes, so before you buy one have some idea of the use you'll put it to. For the large ones, shoulder straps (like you see on backpacks) are a nice feature when you have to haul your gear some distance from the boat to your campsite. Some of the most high-tech bags around are designed to hold cameras. They have features like a bag inside an inflated bag for shock protection or an optically clear plastic front panel so you can shoot pictures with the camera still in the bag. There are also available high-quality, padded rigid containers for cameras and special liners for ammo cans. Cameras and their lenses are often the most valuable and the most fragile pieces of gear on a river trip—rather than leaving them at home, give serious thought to providing them with adequate protection. Finally, a low-cost approach to watertight bags that you see all the time on the river is using heavy duty plastic garbage bags. Put all your gear in one, get most of the air out, then tie it securely (don't use the little plastic clamps or ties that come with the bag). Then put that bag inside another one and tie it off. Now put the whole parcel into a light duffle bag or other cloth bag to protect the waterproof but fragile material of the garbage bags.

Loading Your Boat

If you've got a small, one-man or two-man craft, loading is generally very rapid and simple because as far as volume you are not carrying very much. Put your watertight containers in the extreme stern or bow and make sure they will stay there if you and your boat go upside down. You don't want them to hit or irritate you in any way and you don't want them thrown loose into the river. When lashing them in, be certain that in time of trouble the ropes or straps you use cannot entangle you.

Loading a large raft is a more complicated and tedious chore, simply because you're carrying so much. In all rafts the primary location for gear is behind the boatman. In my raft I also have the space under my seat (I removed the back thwart) and directly behind the passenger seat (in front of the cross support I rest my feet on). I try to avoid all the weight ending up in the rear to be certain that my raft won't be sluggish as I row backwards. In fact, I put the heaviest of the gear behind the passenger seat; that places much of the total weight I'm carrying in the center of the boat, over the raft's pivot point. For a low center of gravity, put the heaviest gear and supplies in first, stacking lighter things on top of them. Typically, all boats carry coolers for cold drinks and perishable foods. I have one that slides under my seat and then a giant one in front of my feet. The one up front is easily accessible to the passengers and the boatman and carries drinks, snacks and lunches. The one under my seat I generally open only in camp, for meals. Both coolers are lashed to the raft frame by their handles.

Once the coolers are in and secure, I load all the lightweight waterproof bags in the space behind the boatman's seat. It is important to systematically and carefully lash them all in, tying to the seat in front and D-rings on the sides and back. Be very certain that the ropes or straps you use can in no way entrap you if you are thrown off your seat or your boat is flipped; check all knots, avoid long loose ends. One system for lashing gear is by using a custom fit piece of heavy nylon netting. It is placed over the entire stern compartment and then snapped or tied to the seat and D-rings. A smaller piece of netting can be used in the same fashion to secure gear behind the passenger seat.

A problem is created when you fill the back end with waterproof bags. They often sit in a few inches of water and it is difficult to bail underneath them. Use of a bilge pump (rather than a bail bucket) helps, but some people approach this problem by elevating the gear a few inches from the raft floor. If you use closed-cell foam under your frame you can extend it into the stern area but it only elevates the gear an inch or two. Some frames have as an option a rigid gear deck extending out behind the boatman which is several inches above the raft floor. Other rafters set the gear onto a hammock-like deck suspended from the seat and surrounding D-rings. I've gotten along for years by bilging as best I can and making certain that all my bags are completely watertight and loaded with the closure end up.

After the coolers and the bulk of your gear is loaded on board, there are usually odds and ends left. Small bags (for cameras, sunglasses, sun hats, and so on) may be lashed to or snapped around the frame to secure them. I have two ammo boxes, one with personal items (extra eyeglasses, pipe tobacco, car keys, fishing license, permit papers, and so on) and one with repair items (extra oarlock, patch kit, tools, and so on). A lot of rafters attach these to the top of their frame, usually ahead of the oarlocks a couple of feet or so. Mine are sitting in aluminum frames (with safety ties) below my seat, on both sides of the cooler. Most boatmen carry an extra oar. There's an ongoing controversy as to how to secure it. The one time I lost an oar in a big rapid, there was no way I could have snatched up another one and put it in the oarlock, no matter how accessible it was (I was too busy keeping the boat from turning sideways). I tie my extra oar securely onto the frame along the outside of the boat. Some rafters, in order to make it more accessible, carry it loose inside the boat or attach it to the frame with quick-release knots or velcro tie-ons. There are significant pros and cons no matter what you decide to do with your back-up oar.

Camping Gear

If you are going to stay overnight along the river it is very important to carefully plan for your comfort and safety. You'll need protection from the elements (beyond clothing concerns, which will be discussed later) and a reasonable level of comfort so you can enjoy getting back on the river tomorrow. Except when assured of no precipitation, minimal wind, and little offensive action from bugs you should carry a tent. The best ones for river running are those used for backpacking; they are durable, water repelling, screened against insects, and very light in weight. Most hold two people comfortably, although some are bigger. Heavy, large cabin tents are reasonable only if you like a lot of people around you at night or insist upon being able to stand upright in your shelter. If you need low cost and minimally adequate protection from rain or snow, you can string a line between two boulders or trees and drape a tarp over it (securing the base with rocks). In rain camping consider taking along another tarp (10 by 12 feet works well) to set up, using oars or paddles as poles, for a kitchen and sitting area.

When the weather is bad and the temperature drops low at night, it is critical that you have a high quality sleeping bag. Again, check out the ones that are made for backpacking. They give the maximum amount of warmth for the minimum amount of weight by using either down or high-tech synthetic insulation (like Quallofil or Polar Guard). I prefer to avoid down-filled bags because of the problems created if they get damp or wet. Consider also some form of padding underneath your bag (it can double as a moisture barrier if you don't use a tent). There are available varying thicknesses and sizes of closed-cell foam pads and several types of air mattresses. The larger inflatable kayaks, when the floor is only moderately inflated, can make a very comfortable bed.

Staying overnight creates the need for light. Flashlights are a necessity for moving around after dark. Consider also a lantern for group use in camp after dark, to supplement the light of the moon and your campfire. In the winter when the days are shorter, a propane or white gas lantern allows a lot of activity that would be difficult with just flashlights for illumination.

Menu

When it comes to meals on the river, there are two extreme schools of thought—"steaks versus seeds." One position advocates at least as fancy if not more elaborate meals than one gets at home in the city. To pull this off, a lot of gear is required, ranging from woks to gas barbeques to corkscrews. Kayakers and canoeists carrying all their own food and gear pretty well have to rule out the "steaks" approach. The other approach to the menu is similar to that of backpackers—simple, low weight, small quantities, heavy on granola and trail mixes, low sugar and high carbohydrate, some of it freeze-dried, and little or no preparation required. A reasonable compromise for river running in big boats, especially on longer trips where weight and space become critical, is a place somewhere between the two extremes. My lunches are generally of the backpacker style—light and healthy, and no preparation or fussing around required. For breakfast, a little work is okay and I like some fruit with whatever we have. On most trips I have been on, if the menu gets elaborate, it's at dinner. I've had everything from broiled filet mignon to lasagna, complete with hors d'oeuvres, salad, vegetables, and dessert. You may be surprised at what cán be accomplished by beginning the preparation at home. A great omelet for fourteen can be created in camp by carrying one plastic bottle full of shelled eggs and another full of diced meat, peppers, and mushrooms. I've had pre-cooked (then frozen prior to the

Low Weight Foods

BREAKFAST

Instant Hot Cereals	Instant Pancakes
Breakfast Bars	Cold Cereal/Powdered Milk
Freeze-dried Breakfasts	Instant Breakfast/Powdered Milk
Dried Fruit	Eggs (pre-shelled or powdered)
Toast and Honey	Canned Bacon
Granola (hot or cold)	English Muffins and Jam

LUNCH

Snack Foods (cheese, salami, crackers, etc.)	Beef Jerky
	Meat Sticks
Trail Mixes (nuts, raisins, seeds, etc.)	Granola Bars
Citrus Fruit (pre-peeled, pre-sliced oranges, tangerines, etc.)	Simple sandwiches (canned tuna, peanut butter, cheese, etc.)
Chips (corn or potato)	

DINNER

Freeze-dried Dinners	One-pot Stews (canned meats, dried
Spaghetti (pré-cooked sauce)	vegetables, noodles, powdered
Omelet (pre-shelled eggs, pre-diced meats and vegetables)	sauces, instant soup, etc., all combined)
Lightweight Fresh Vegetables	Sloppy Joe's (toast and meat sauce)
Submarine Sandwiches	

trip) shrimp casserole that tasted like it came from a fine French res-
taurant. Spaghetti usually shows up at least once on most of my
multi-day runs; it's pretty easy if you pre-cook the sauce and just
have to heat it up and boil the noodles. Always popular in camp are
various soups and stews, a great place for your imagination, for your
personal touch. Over the past several years Dutch ovens have become
a popular piece of kitchen equipment, primarily because if you know
how to use them you can cook virtually anything in camp along the
river that you choose. There are numerous books available on their
care and use.

Kitchen Gear

Presuming you don't have all pre-prepared, cold foods you'll need
some kitchen gear. I carry a two-burner white gas stove and the fuel
to run it. For river runners in small boats, miniature stoves made for
backpackers are an alternative (I also carry one of these, for backup
and for coffee). Of course, make sure you've got matches or a lighter
to start your stove. For rafting cookware a Dutch oven, a large frying
pan, and a couple of pots pretty well cover all bases. A large spoon,
a spatula, and a potholder are common accessories. Also consider
bringing a coffee pot and a can opener, depending on your group and
the trip's menu. As part of the kitchen or as part of each individual's
personal gear, you should carry bowls and/or plates, and knife, fork,
spoon and cup. When equippping your kitchen, look at your menu.
Make sure you've got all the gear necessary to put your planned meals
together.

Dinner preparation in camp.

Clothing

I consider clothing in three categories: For the river, for the camp, and in the event of precipitation. Your *river clothes* will vary depending on the temperature of the air and the water. The simplest condition is when both are warm. You'll need a pair of river shoes, some you don't care if you ruin by repeated soaking. Running shoes are the best. They are fairly durable in river running conditions and most have a lug-type tread design which is good for traction in the boat and on the bank. Thongs and other forms of sandals are not recommended; they may not stay on when you really need them. The rest of your hot weather river outfit can consist of a swimsuit, or shorts and a T-shirt. Remember that in very hot sun, dark colors absorb heat while light colors reflect it.

For rafting, if your day's float is a long one, consider jogging type pants and a windbreaker top. Made of quick-drying nylon, they will give some protection from wind and sun. For early morning and early evening warm-up, you can slip on light sweatpants and sweatshirts or sweater under them. Any time you have to spend long hours in the sun, bring a hat. They make caps for river running with extra large bills and flaps down the back to keep the sun off your neck. Ordinary baseball-style caps work pretty well. I like broad brimmed straw hats, but they have one distinct problem. Water rapidly causes them to lose their shape and they get pitched in the river quite easily by gusts of wind.

If you want to run rivers when the air and the water are not warm, your clothing must be more elaborate. Put on wool socks under your river shoes—wool maintains most of its insulating qualities when wet. Some people, especially those in smaller and wetter boats, prefer wet suit socks to keep their feet dry as well as warm. Then wear lightweight warm clothes, looking to wool or pile as two popular options. Consider long underwear, made from wool or the synthetic polypropylene. Particularly avoid cottons (including jeans) for river running, for once they get wet, wind hitting them will accelerate rather than prevent chill. In order to keep dry and add even more insulation, you can cover your whole outfit with a rain suit or poncho. Finally, either as a protection against blisters or for warmth, some boatmen wear gloves (usually made of leather).

If you're running a river with cold water, even sitting in a raft you must consider a *wet suit*. If you are in a small boat, it is not optional— you'll be wet and chilling (or worse) most of the trip without it. From any size of craft, if pitched into a cold river you risk drowning when the effects of hypothermia prevent you safely getting to shore (see Chapter IX). Wet suits have been a mainstay for river running for years; made of stretchy neoprene, they have been the only dependable protection from hypothermia when immersed in cold water. They offer insulation from the cold by holding a thin layer of water between you and the suit, a layer that is warmed by your body. The chill of the river is thus kept from direct contact with your skin and the loss of your body heat is minimized. This latter fact explains the overheating that can occur if you wear a wetsuit on hot days. Wet

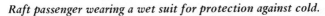

Raft passenger wearing a wet suit for protection against cold.

suits vary in thickness, but most used by river runners are 1/8 inch thick. Popular with paddlers are "Farmer John" styles, suits without shoulders or sleeves (for ease of movement). Paddle jackets can be added when you need to cover your whole upper body. Also available are full single-piece suits, shirts, and pants (including thigh-covering shorts), socks or booties, boots, and gloves. Recent technology has allowed a rapid popularity surge in the drysuit as a direct competitor with the wet suit. However, they tend to be considerably more expensive. They are typically made of polyurethane coated fabric with rubberized seals around the neck, wrists, and ankles. Instead of a layer of water as an insulator, wool or polypropylene underwear is usually worn under them (and it will remain dry).

In selecting *camp clothes* for your trip, temperature is again an important factor. When you get off the river in warm weather, chances are it'll cool down quite a bit before you crawl into your sleeping bag. You need dry, warm clothes and shoes or boots to replace your soggy river attire. Bring long pants and a warm, long-sleeve sweater or jacket. If you are floating in a cold time of the year, then look into long underwear, down parkas or vests, wool pants, and so on. Consider using your rain gear as the outermost layer because of its heat retaining qualities. Better overkill on clothes than sitting around all evening shivering. And remember, tomorrow you will have to get back into your river clothes; take the time and effort to make certain they will be dry by morning.

As has been evident from the above discussion, *rain clothes* are useful not only to repel water but also for keeping your body heat losses to a minimum. Rain gear is usually one of two types, either a densely rubberized material or one of the new high-tech, "breathing" coated fabrics (like Gortex, Bion II, or Entrant). Both work okay, but my medium heavy, "rubber" coat and pants are particularly rugged and durable, and not very expensive. Instead of coat and pants, a long poncho is a good alternative for camp use. If you are preparing for a rainy camp, be certain that your shoes or boots are water resistant and that you have a rain hat.

River Campsite

Once everything is loaded in your boats, you spend the day on the river. It's getting well into the afternoon, time to start thinking about camp. On some rivers, there are campsites virtually everywhere. On other rivers, they are few and far between. There are several things to consider when choosing a campsite. On some rivers, for some floaters, the number one variable is whether there are toilet facilities. Other factors people consider include creeks (preferably

with clean enough water to drink), space (sufficient to spead out
your whole group), shade from the sun, contour (flat, preferably soft
sand or grass, for sleeping), and sound (a nearby rapid or babbling
brook to lull you to sleep). A lot of times you can't get all this, so be
willing to prioritize and compromise. Finally, take care in securing
your boats at whatever campsite you choose. If possible, pick them
up and bring them well up onto shore, especially for rivers which can
readily change level overnight. If you leave them partly in the water,
always carefully secure them by their bowlines. Also, be aware that
wave action can rub your boat all night against nearby rocks—if you
are not careful you could have some patching to do in the morning.

Environmental Impact

One of the major reasons people run rivers, especially those who
seek extended trips, is to "get back to nature." It's disgusting to
make a drive from the city, float all day deep into a wilderness, and
then step out of your boat to empty beer cans, discarded wrappers,
and cigarette butts. A basic rule of river camping is to leave nothing
behind but your footprints (wind and water will erase them). Sometimes this is a difficult rule to follow to the letter, but if you work at
it you can achieve it. After you leave your campsite, you've suc-
ceeded in low impact camping if the next group there can't tell you
preceded them.

Whenever possible camp below the high water mark. Rocky or
sandy bars are particularly good because there's little damage that
can be done that the spring flood waters won't erase (and sand or
very fine gravel is particularly pleasant under your body at night). If
you cannot camp below the high water mark, or need to go above it
for protection from the elements, tread especially lightly on that
environment. Don't dig, cut, trample or otherwise affect the existing
ecology unless absolutely necessary, and then keep it to a minimum.
And in your attention to low impact camping, keep in mind that you
should not impact on the river either. Basically, don't put anything
in the river other than your boat and occasionally, if you want or
can't avoid it, your body. I was part of a day trip one time for a
dozen emotionally disturbed teenagers. One of the boatmen flipped
over two dozen filtertip cigarette butts into the water during the
float. A paddler in an inflatable kayak carefully collected virtually
all of them throughout the day and then just before the take-out
tossed them all over the floor in the offending boatman's raft. Sadly
enough, a lot of floaters pitch their garbage into the water. When in
camp the major polluting occurs around cleaning (kitchen gear and

people). To fully present the notion of low environmental impact, several specific areas are discussed below in detail.

Campfires

One of the standard unsightly scars in many river campsites are fire rings with half-burnt wood and ashes. In some locations this is becoming such a problem that once white sandy beaches now appear grey or black. Many protected rivers are now requiring *firepans.* To add to the problem, popular campsites often are surrounded by half-broken, partially sawed trees, the result of scrounging for firewood.

Warmth on a cold evening around a firepan campfire.

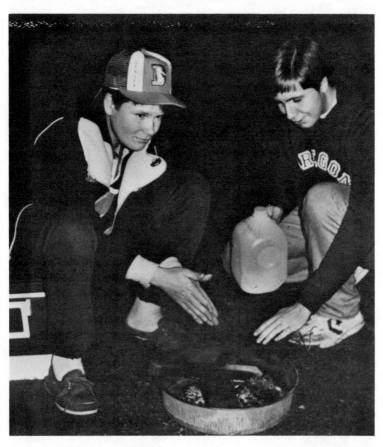

Consider not having a fire, other than the one produced by your stove. If you must build a fire for protection from the elements or cooking, bring a firepan. A firepan is simply a metal container with 5 or 6 inch high sides to serve as your fire ring. There are commercially manufactured ones with grills, upright hangers for pots, adjustable vents, and so on. A popular low-cost alternative is a large oil pan. Whatever kind you use, elevate it on rocks so it won't scorch the earth below it. Keep the fire small enough to be contained easily within the pan. If you're running a popular stretch of river, consider bringing firewood from home or picking up driftwood along the day's float to avoid having to scour an already well-picked over campsite.

The only problem created by firepans is what to do with the ashes. The best alternative is to cool them (with water) and carry them out (a good container is an old ammo can). Some floaters use them the next evening for a bed for their next fire. On some rivers it has been recommended that fine ashes be dropped into the river in heavy current (not into slow current or eddies where they will just wash right back to shore).

On those emergency occasions when you must build a fire without a pan, make a small one and do so if possible below the high water mark. Also if possible, it should be made on gravel or sand or bare dirt. Before you leave, try to destroy all indications of your fire. You can collect the ashes and throw scorched rocks into the river. For any fire, in a firepan or not, be alert to the dangers of blowing sparks and coals. Avoid building it near pine needles, dried grasses, and in any other place where there's a risk of setting the campsite on fire. Since you'll need it for dousing your campfire at some point anyway, have a couple of containers of water nearby, just in case.

Camp Garbage

Inevitably, camping people produce garbage—metal cans, paper wrappers, plastic bags, uneaten food, and so on. The basic rule is "bag it up and carry it out." You can reduce the bulk by burning what you can in your firepan and crushing the rest. The best container is a heavy duty garbage bag (or two, one inside the other) inside a cloth bag (old duffle bag, burlap gunny sack, or whatever). And don't believe those who say it's acceptable to pitch leftover edibles alongside the camp. It will attract flies and other insects as well as encouraging camp-raiding animals. In campsites with outhouses, don't use them for garbage. Your garbage will prevent the decomposition of human waste as well as fill them up sooner than is really necessary.

Washing

A common camp activity is washing—teeth, bodies, plates, cook-pots, and so on. It's not uncommon to see floaters standing waist deep in the river lathering themselves up with ordinary household bath soap, then dunking to rinse. This is another form of throwing garbage in the river. If you want to shower, take biodegradable soap and some containers full of water well above the high water line, find a bare or rocky place, and clean yourself there. If you bring a friend to dump the water over you, all the better. While camping on the river consider brushing your teeth with a bare minimum of tooth-paste, again above the high water line.

Washing the after-dinner pots, pans, plates, cups, and so on, is somewhat more complicated. Not only do you want them cosmeti-cally clean, but to prevent intestinal problems, you want to disinfect them. Many campers run their wash through two or three stages. The first is always a scrub in very hot water laced with biodegradable dishwashing soap. The second step is a steaming hot rinse. Some people like a third step, a rinse through a bucket of cold water with a capful of ordinary household bleach in it. The water from step one is usually pretty dirty and should be disposed of well above the high water mark. Dig a shallow hole for it if it has a lot of solids, then cover it up.

Human Waste

There are two approaches to the problem of human waste (feces), latrines and portable toilets, when outhouses are not available. Urina-tion generally does not present problems—just find a place above the high water line. Many protected rivers have now regulated against dug-out latrines. Some popular campsites have hundreds of latrines, some of them very poorly conceived, and the whole place literally stinks. If you are going to use a latrine, dig a trench (the length will vary de-pending on the number of people in your party) about 10 to 12 inches deep. If you dig it too deep, decomposition will not occur very rapid-ly. Toilet paper is much slower to break down than feces. Use thin, cheap paper or that made especially for camping, and light it on fire after use (or carry it out in plastic bags). Do not deposit feminine hygiene products in the latrine; they are extremely resistant to de-composition and should be carried out.

A more environmentally sound approach to human waste is a por-table latrine, so you can carry everything out. They are available commercially or can be fashioned from a toilet seat and large ammo box or similar leak-proof container. You can use chemicals (like formaldehyde) to disinfect them. Many people prefer to avoid chemicals; they simply want to catch human waste (and sanitary napkins, tampons, and so on) in airtight plastic bags, then seal them. One approach is to have fifteen or twenty small, thin garbage bags lining a container, one inside the other, open and attached at the toilet seat. After you go, tie up the top of your bag (the innermost one) securely, lift it out and place it in a container that's used to transport all the used bags. This second container should be airtight and doubly lined with thick garbage bags.

Wildlife

The final comments in this chapter on river camping are about wildlife. If you're floating wilderness or near-wilderness you will undoubtedly encounter animal wildlife. Recognize that you are a visitor in their home, and for them as well as for all the other reasons discussed in this section, do not disturb it. Discourage camp scrounging both by leaving a garbage-free campsite and by resisting the temptation to feed them while you eat. You are markedly affecting their ability to fend for themselves by sharing your meals with them. Be especially alert to not disturbing burrows, nests, dens, and so on. And certainly don't attack the animals you see—not with a gun, or sticks, or rocks, or whatever. Assume an attitude of peaceful coexistence, and except for a rare camp-raiding bear or camp-diving bird, everyone including the local creatures will benefit.

Chapter 8

Fishing Techniques

MANY OF OUR NATION'S BEST WHITEWATER RIVERS are also some of our best fishing rivers. At certain times of year on many of them you'll see more drift boats full of fishermen than rafts, kayaks, and so on, combined. They will be clustered between the big rapids and in the middle of some of the smaller ones, systematically working holes, channels and drifts. And for floaters whose primary focus is not fishing, many like to toss a line in at camp, trying to catch a fresh dinner or just wile away an hour or two relaxing on a rock.

General Facts

If you intend to fish, you need to know what kind of fish inhabit the river you're going to run and when. The most popular species for whitewater fishermen is trout. For many of the rivers that run to the sea, steelhead (essentially a trout that has migrated downriver, into the ocean, and now a few years later is back in the river headed upstream to spawn) fishing prevails. Also available, depending on the river, are other fish such as catfish, carp, shad, perch, bass, and several varieties of salmon. The focus of this chapter will be on trout and steelhead, although some of the techniques described work well for other species of fish.

For a lot of rivers, especially those flowing into the ocean, it is important to know when to fish. Typically, trout are dumped in from a hatchery upstream and move toward the coast, creating a "run." However, some fish are generally available in most rivers all year (of course, in land-locked rivers the trout can't disappear into the ocean). Steelhead make runs up ocean-linked rivers at fairly predictable times each year. For example, the Rogue River in Oregon has a summer-fall run with fish averaging 2 or 3 pounds, the height of which reaches the Grants Pass area in late September. A smaller (in numbers of fish) winter run follows it, reaching a peak around February, with the steelhead averaging 6 to 7 pounds. The early summer months have no steelhead, but June and July is a great time to catch pan-sized hatchery trout. If you need to know what's in any river at any particular time of year, check with local tackle shops or sporting goods stores.

River Features

Whether fishing from the bank or your boat, certain features of the river indicate a greater likelihood of catching a fish; that is, trout and steelhead spend most of their time in particular parts of the river and stay away from others. For example, it's rare to hook one (especially steelhead) in completely still water or in very shallow water or in extremely deep water. There are several features you should look for because your chances of hooking a fish are much increased: a) Moving water that's from 3 to 15 feet deep (generally closer to 15 feet for bigger steelhead); b) the last 20 to 60 feet of the smooth water just before a rapid; c) a tailout, after the big waves; d) "slots" or channels (a narrow stretch of water, often along a steep bank, that is deeper than the rest of the river); e) a riffle (used here to mean a 3 to 6 foot deep stretch of fast, bubbly water); and f) next to boulders and ledges (including submerged ones) in medium fast water. One of the best ways to learn where to catch fish is to take a day trip in a drift boat with an experienced commercial fishing guide. They not only should be expert at negotiating whitewater, but should be equally as skilled at catching fish. Also consider going along with an "old-timer," an experienced local fisherman, or visiting with the clerks at a local sporting goods store or tackle shop where you purchase your license. Ask them the questions you have about fishing the river you are going to run.

Equipment

Before moving to a discussion of specific fishing techniques, some comments should be made about rods and reels. Most rod manufacturers make *rods* specifically for trout and/or steelhead fishing—they are generally quite strong but very lively (especially at the tip) and between 6 and 9 feet long. Use the longer ones for steelhead (or fly fishing), the shorter ones for trout, the middle lengths for both (7 or 7½ feet is an ideal compromise length).

The most popular reel on whitewater rivers is the *spinning reel*. Its major advantage is ease of casting; some other advantages are its resistance to snarling the line and the fact that you can push a button and reel backwards to let out more line after the cast (to cover more water while maintaining tension on the line). Its major disadvantage is seen in twisted line, which occurs from turning the handle when a fish or snag is not retrieving. Steadily growing in popularity among experienced fishermen is the new breed of *level wind reels* now available, made specifically for bank fishing. Level winds have been around for about as long as anyone can remember, but the new ones have fancy "cast control systems" built in which have cut down on that type of reel's very frustrating disadvantage—the backlash (the "bird's nest," horrendous snarling of your line on the reel's spool). If you learn to handle these new reels, you can cast further, retrieve more rapidly, have better control of the drag (resistance to outgoing line), and never worry about twisting your line. Also, if you use approaches to fishing that don't involve casting (most of these techniques are done from a boat), the level wind reel is more suitable than a spinning reel. This is primarily true because of the added control you have for feeding line out.

Fishing Reels

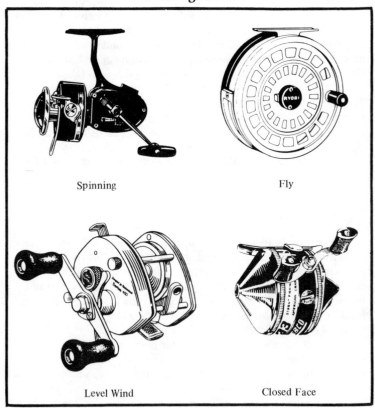

Spinning

Fly

Level Wind

Closed Face

The other two types of reels you'll see on the river are the closed-face (Zebco type) and fly reels. A *closed-face reel* is just that—the spool holding the line is enclosed and in the middle of the face of that enclosure is a hole where line comes out. Most people think of these reels as being only for beginners, because they are often very inexpensive and are virtually snarl-proof. However, for people who prefer the closed-face reel, there are high capacity, high quality versions available. Most of the *fly reels* you'll see are being used by fly fishermen on the bank; however, they also work well for boat fishing, trolling techniques. Some commercial guides prefer them because of the simplicity of the reel and the fact that beginners using them rarely snarl the line or "horse" the fish in (bring it in too rapidly).

Once you've invested in a quality rod and reel which suits your fishing needs and preferences, don't buy cheap *line*. Invest in quality line—it's the only thing between you and your fish. Lines are rated as to the number of pounds they will support. Generally, for trout use 4 to 6 pound test, for steelhead use 6 to 15 pound test, with 6 or 8 pound being the best compromise if you're fishing for both at the same time. Also, look to quality for anything you attach to your line, like hooks, swivels, snaps, and leader. It can be upsetting and frustrating to see a 10 pound steelhead resume its migration because your tackle failed.

Bank Fishing

There are a number of different ways to go about fishing from the bank. No matter what technique you use, someone will suggest another one if you're not catching fish (and sometimes, when you are). Discussed below are four popular, well-proven approaches to fishing for trout and steelhead—plunking, drifting, floating, and hydroplaning. If you are a beginner, follow the details carefully and then as you gain experience make the modifications you like for particular rivers, sizes of fish, climate, tackle innovations, and so on.

Plunking

Plunking refers to still fishing where a heavy weight is used to keep bait from moving downstream with the current. A typical rig uses heavy line, 10 to 20 pound test, tied to one of the opposing loops of a triple (3-ended) swivel. A 1 to 4 ounce weight, depending on the speed of the current, is tied to the odd end of the swivel with 4 or 5 inches of 4 to 8 pound test leader (heavier leader with heavier line).

Floating Whitewater Rivers

In the event of a serious snag, the light leader will break and you will lose only the weight. Connect a size 2 (large steelhead) to size 12 (small trout) bait hook for worms, or a 3/0 (large steelhead) to size 4 (trout) egg type hook with an egg loop tied into the leader for roe, to the third swivel end with about 2 feet of leader. To fish single eggs, use a regular size 8 or size 10 hook. The leader should be lighter than your line. Some fishermen prefer to use an ordinary two-ended swivel

Knots for Fishermen

INCH KNOT
(for joining line to line or line to leader)

BLOOD KNOT 1
(for joining line to line or leader to leader)

BLOOD KNOT 2
(for joining two lines of unequal diameter or line to leader)

PALOMAR KNOT
(for tying hook, swivel or lure to line or leader)

DOUBLE EYE KNOT
(for tying on hooks)

DOUBLE LOOP CLINCH KNOT
(for tying on swivels)

END LOOP KNOT
(to form an attachment loop)

SIMPLE LOOP KNOT
(to form an attachment loop)

for connecting line to leader and have the weight attached (again by 4 or 5 inches of light leader) to a second swivel which slides freely on the line above the first swivel. This rigging gives a better "feel" of strikes as the fish does not have to drag the weight around. Plunking is best done in the slow water alongside of fast current or in channels with very slow moving, fairly deep water. Wait patiently for a fish to attack or nibble your bait—when you think a fish has his mouth over your hook, grab the rod and pull back sharply (move the rod tip 2 to 3 feet) to set the hook. Steelhead, especially the big ones, may give just a little "tug" on the line, while trout bites often feel like something pecking on the bait. For both, if you're lucky, they'll gobble it and set the hook themselves. When the action is slow, retrieve your rig every few minutes to check your bait and/or change location slightly.

Drift Fishing

The most popular way to fish a river from the bank is drift fishing. You can use bait or lures for this style of fishing. Most tackle shops have a wide selection of lures, varying as to design and size—choose the ones best suited to the kind and size of fish you're after. Standing on the bank or wading out in shallow water, cast well into the current and a little upstream (the faster the water, the further upstream). Allow the bait or lure to drop near the bottom of the river and be carried downstream. At the end of the drift the bait or lure will swing around to the bank—reel it in, at first very slowly, and cast again. When drift fishing there is often a possibility of snagging the bottom if you are doing it correctly. You must fish near the bottom to have the best chance of hooking a fish, especially a steelhead. Experienced anglers "walk" their weight downstream with a gentle up and down motion of the rod tip. If you snag, pull sharply as if setting the hook in a fish (it's always possible that what you thought was the bottom is actually a large fish). If a few sharp snaps do not free it, try changing your location on the bank (walk upstream) or letting out several feet of slack and then reeling up rapidly. When nothing else works, wrap the line around your hand or arm, taking care not to cut yourself with it, and walk away from the river—be prepared to lose at least part of your rig. Anytime you snag, it's always a good idea to check your gear for damage, especially the hook.

When drifting, be sure to often change the length of your cast (the fish may be right at your feet or clear on the other side of the river) and your position on the bank. This will allow you to cover more water. There are several ways to rig up for drifting including the

Four Ways to Rig for Drifting Bait

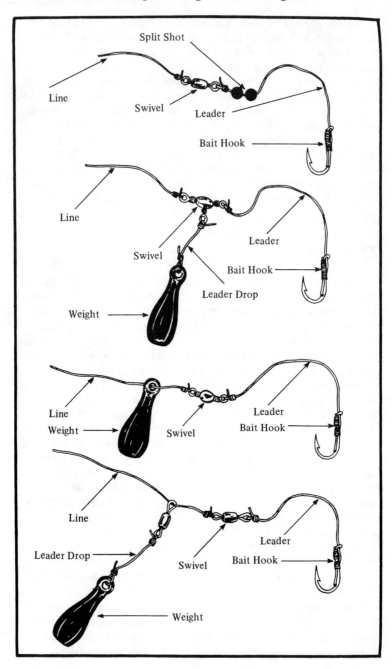

Line and Leader Combination for Drifting Bait

FISH	WEIGHT	LENGTH	LINE	LEADER
Small trout	Under 1/2 lb.	Under 10 in.	4 lb.	1 lb.
Medium Trout	1/2 to 1 lb.	10 to 15 in.	4 lb.	1 or 2 lb.
Large Trout and Small Steelhead	1 to 3 lbs.	15 to 20 in.	6 lb.	3 or 4 lb.
Giant Trout and Medium Steelhead	3 to 8 lbs.	20 to 30 in.	10 lb.	6 or 8 lb.
Large Steelhead	8 to 15 lbs.	30 to 36 in.	15 lb.	10 or 12 lb.
Giant Steelhead	Over 15 lbs.	Over 36 in.	20 lb.	15 lb.

same as for plunking, but use considerably less weight (usually from 1/8 to 1/2 ounce, depending on the speed and depth of the water) and lighter line and leader. Generally, go with as light as tackle as is reasonable to assure low visibility to the fish. Some fishermen prefer to just use a split shot or two clamped to the leader near the swivel for weight. Also very popular is pencil shaped lead which is rigged by using an inch or so of surgical tubing to hold it, or in a hollow form which can be crimped to hold it on your 4 or 5 inch leader drop. If you are fishing lures, no weight is required. Also, if your line is fairly light you don't need leader either; just tie the line directly to the ring on the lure. Avoid swivels anywhere in the rigging because they can disturb the action of the lure. If you want to be able to easily switch lures, a small snap (not snap swivel) can be tied to the end of the line.

Drifting: Cover the Water

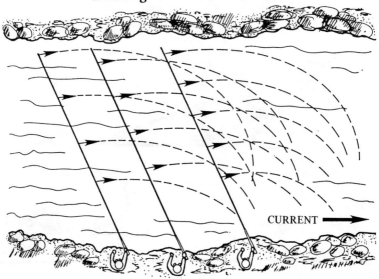

CURRENT ➡

Floating Flies

Floating approaches are generally reserved for artificial flies or live insects, like grasshoppers. This can be done using traditional fly fishing equipment and casting techniques. Contrary to other forms of casting where you fling weight at the end of your line out into the river, in classic fly fishing you are literally casting the line. To cast the line (which has at the end of it a virtually weightless leader and artificial insect) it requires skills not needed for the other techniques presented in this chapter. This is probably the most difficult form of fishing to learn to do correctly—you'll want expert personal assistance to get you started off right.

There is a relatively easy approach to floating which seems to be growing in popularity (especially for trout fishing), utilizing a clear plastic bubble. Designed for casting, it provides weight yet floats on top of the water. The large end of the bubble is tied to the line; tie 3 to 5 feet of 2 or 3 pound test leader to the small end of the bubble; tie a fly (or bait hook and live insect) to the free end of the leader. Cast the rig well out into the river and let it float downstream and swing around to the bank, then cast again. As with drift fishing, vary the length of the cast and your position on the bank to cover more water. Some fishermen like to "twitch" the fly (little pulls on the rod every few seconds) as it is floating to attract the fish's attention. The floating fly technique generally is most productive early in the morning and during the last hour of daylight in the evening, in shallow little riffles.

Casting: Bubble

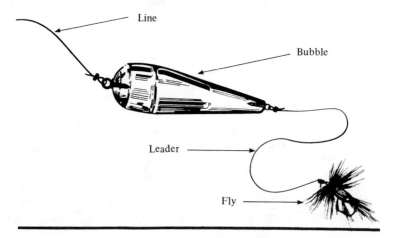

Line

Bubble

Leader

Fly

Hydroplaning

An approach to bank fishing that has recently been gaining in popularity among steelheaders, one that works for all sizes of fish, is hydroplaning lures. Like plunking, it's a relatively low energy approach to catching fish, one that's very compatible with relaxing with a good book or discussing the day's rapids with your fellow floaters. Also, in some rivers, you'll have a good chance of hooking a salmon this way. This technique requires the use of an odd looking plastic device called by various names such as "hydroplane" or "aquakite" or "side planer" or "poor man's drift boat." Using this remarkable device a bank fisherman can hold a lure in a steady position way out in midstream! To rig a hydroplane use a rod that is reasonably stiff and preferably a level wind reel. It is common to use heavy line (15 to 20 pound test) to be certain you don't lose your hydroplane. Thread the line through the eye on the hydroplane (according to the instructions that come with the device) and tie on a swivel. On the other end of the swivel tie on 5 or 6 feet of much lighter leader. You finish the rigging by tying a diving lure (like a Hot Shot or a Wee Wart) onto the free end of the leader. You must use a diving lure to make sure you are fishing near the bottom. As the hydroplane holds your lure steady in midstream, the river's current causes it to dive downward toward the bottom. To launch the hydroplaning rig,

The key to starting a hydroplane is to carefully set it into mild downstream current.

you'll need a little moving water at your feet—lay the hydroplane and its trailing lure gently into the water and the river will do the rest. When fish hit a diving lure, they generally nail it and setting the hook is not an issue. It is also possible to fish bait with a hydroplane. Instead of a diving lure, you can attach a specially made diving device which is designed to tow bait hooks with worms or eggs. With this rigging, you may have to set the hook when you feel a strong tug.

Landing the Fish

The final topic to be addressed for bank fishing is that of playing the fish, once he's hooked. For smaller fish, you generally can just reel them in. Larger fish, however, have an extensive bag of tricks to select from for getting loose—long runs into heavy current, spinning in circles, tail-dancing, swimming toward you, playing dead, leaping out of the water, and so on. No matter what techniques you use to get a fish on the line, there are three basic things to remember if you want to see it on the dinner table. Number one rule: Keep your rod tip up, don't point it at the fish! Your rod will act like a shock absorber, so the fish never gets a solid tub or snap on your line, leader, and the knots that hold everything together. Number two: Always keep the line taut—give your fish slack and you double his chances of getting away. If he comes toward you fast, reel in as rapidly as you can and hope for the best. And rule number three: Don't "horse" your fish, take plenty of time and let the big ones get tired before you try to bring them close. With patience, it's amazing how large a fish can be landed with very light tackle. Recently on a drift on the McKenzie River in Oregon, I was flagged down by a bank fisherman. He was fishing with a 6-foot, ultralight rod, very small reel, and 4 pound test line. In search of trout he had hooked an 18 pound steelhead. I loaded him up in my drift boat and helped him chase his fish for three-quarters of an hour until we finally tired and netted the steelhead. Even tired, expect your fish to make one last wild attempt to free himself when he sees you (and your net). Finally, net him carefully, making certain to be swift and sure—many a fish, even tired ones, have been lost by poor netting. If you are not carrying a net, flip small fish onto the bank with a swift sure motion. Large fish, when very tired, can be grabbed next to the tail or flipped onto shore with your foot.

Before you ever begin fishing, decide if you intend to keep the fish you catch. If you do not plan to cook them right away, you'll need room in your cooler for storage (unless the air temperature is very cool). If you do not intend to keep your catch, consider using barbless hooks; that way you are generally assured of being able to release the fish unharmed. If you don't have barbless hooks, you can file or cut off the large barb at the tip to make regular hooks work quite adequately.

Boat Fishing

You can fish from about anything that will float through the whitewater. However, the best by far is the drift boat. They have plenty of room for people and gear, come with a variety of padded and swivel seats for passenger comfort, and generally are dry for everyone through all but the biggest rapids. Most important though is their ease of handling, for holding in a hole, making a very slow drift down a slot, rowing upstream to try the hot spot again, and so on. I've caught fish out of both rafts and drift boats, and in a raft it's a lot harder work for any of the techniques where you have to hold the boat. All the various ways people fish out of boats can be described in three sections—moving bank, trolling, and floating boat techniques.

Moving Bank

Some floaters basically use their boat only to get to one place and stop, and then move to another. I was on a stretch of the Sandy River (near Portland, Oregon) where fishing from a boat was prohibited. The float allowed you to stop at numerous points along both shorelines, some inaccessible by vehicle or foot. Once you park your boat, the techniques described in the previous section on bank fishing are used. Some fishermen, where fishing from a boat is legal, move from place to place using their anchor to stop their downstream progress alongside of good fishing spots. Again, they typically use bank fishing techniques, especially drifting bait or a lure. When anchored in the river it is possible also to use the trolling techniques discussed below.

Trolling

To put your boat to its maximum advantage over hiking down to a spot along the bank, you not only can cover several miles of water but can systematically cover every square foot you choose to, by trolling. The three most popular approaches to river trolling are pulling diving lures, dragging flies, and "bouncing" bait on the bottom.

Pulling diving lures behind your boat is an art, requiring both know-ledge of where to find fish and an ability to gently handle your oars. Attach the lure directly to your line (10 or 12 pound test for medium size fish), or use a non-swiveling snap if you want to be able to easily change lures. Once you select a spot to fish, about 40 to 50 feet above it instruct your fishing passengers to set their lures gently in the water (to avoid tangling) and let out line. Depending on the boatman and the depth and speed of the water, the amount of line varies. Minimal-ly, let out 30 to 40 feet. It's rare to see anyone out more than 60 or 70 feet—it becomes hard for the boatman to keep track of where your lure is after that. Once the line is out, the passengers need to

Trolling: Cover the Water

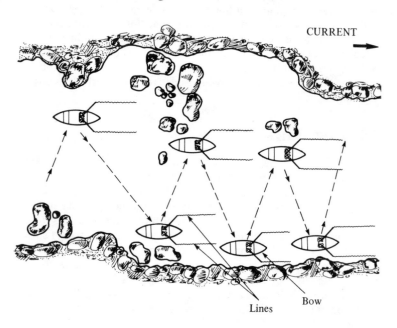

CURRENT

Lines

Bow

keep their rod tips up and be alert to fouling of their lure by sticks, moss, or whatever. Fouling is generally recognized by a cessation of the regular vibration of the rod tip created by the lures diving and wobbling action, or by a lure floating up to the surface. Sometimes a fouled lure can be cleaned off by a sharp snap of the rod; be sure the lure is under the surface of the water when you snap or it may come flying through the air at you. Several years ago boatmen invented a system for trolling diving plugs with bait following. They put a diving lure on the line as usual, but took off all the hooks. Then they tied a 3 or 4 foot leader to the front hook eye on the lure. At the end of the leader they added a hook and bait. The hookless plug keeps the bait near the bottom. As mentioned earlier, a gadget that works the same as the hookless diving lure is now available commercially at most tackle shops.

The real expertise in this approach to fishing is in the hands of the boatman. Starting well above the hole he will work the boat side to side slowly downstream through it. He needs to slow his progress enough that the lures "work" (dive deeply, best determined by watching the vibrating rod tips) and be alert to rocks, possibility of tangling lines, cross currents, and so on. A good commercial fishing guide is a pleasure to watch as he deftly covers every last square inch of a hot spot, carefully laying the lures in alongside of boulders, through channels next to the bank, and other places he's hooked fish before. Once a fish is hooked (they tend to really nail diving lures, eliminating the need for setting the hook) if possible, get the boat to shore or anchored to make playing and netting large fish easier. The only exception is when a large one heads downstream into the next rapid. When the fish has the force of strong current with him, you often have to chase him to the base of the whitewater with your boat. The chance of dragging him back upstream through a rapid is pretty slim.

Using essentially the same rowing techniques described above, you can drag flies behind your boat. This technique is particularly good for trout and small steelhead in the early morning or just before dark. Tie a floating fly onto the end of light line and let the current take it 30 to 50 feet downstream from your boat. Sometimes it's a little more productive if the fly is a foot or two under the water; you can achieve that by putting a split shot or two 24 to 30 inches from the fly. Some fishermen recommend twitching the line every few seconds to make a more natural and attention-getting presentation. You can use live insects instead of artificial flies if they are available. The boatman should look for shallow (3 to 6 feet deep), bubbly water and cover it completely.

For the third trolling technique, bouncing the bottom, it is best if the boat is anchored directly upstream of the hole or channel you want to fish. Here's chance for the boatman to fish—although it is possible if you use a rod holder for your rod, the other trolling techniques are best left to the passengers. Bouncing the bottom is a bait-fishing (eggs or worms) technique, best suited to large fish (including salmon), and is sometimes tough for people to catch on to. Use a medium stiff rod, a level wind reel, and 8 to 15 pound test line, rigging essentially like for plunking as described earlier. An important factor in your tackle is a rigging system allowing easy change of weight size—depending on the speed of the current and depth of the river, I've used weights varying from 1/2 ounce up to 4 or 5 ounces. Depending on where you anchor, sometimes you have to change weight even when you fish the other side of the boat.

Begin the bouncing the bottom approach to fishing by holding the rod tip out over the water, your thumb on the spool of line, and then set your reel to free spool (there is a lever or button that eliminates all resistance to outgoing line). Take your thumb off the line and allow the weight (and bait) to drop rapidly to the bottom of the river. At the moment it hits bottom (you can feel it thump, your rod tip will make one small bounce, and you'll have a momentary bit of slack in your line), replace your thumb on the spool of line. From this beginning you are ready to bounce the bottom, slowly working your weight and bait downstream from the boat. Lift your rod tip a foot or two (which picks up your weight off the bottom), then release your thumb pressure a moment so the current can take line and carry the weight downstream until it hits bottom again; when it hits bottom put your thumb back on the spool. Each "pick up, release line, hit bottom" maneuver allows your bait to move downstream. Properly done, you can cover (in a straight line) up to 50 or 60 feet of river.

Bouncing the Bottom

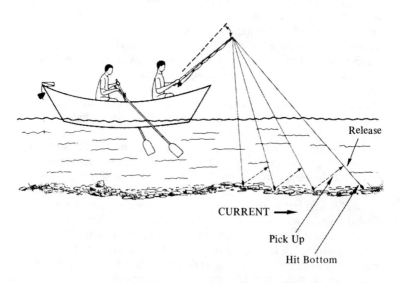

Release

CURRENT →

Pick Up

Hit Bottom

Fishing by bouncing the bottom takes a little practice. Some people have difficulty "feeling" their weight hitting the bottom or controlling the spool (line) with their thumb. If you use this technique, don't rush. Take your time working your way downstream, giving your prospective dinner an opportunity to look over the bait. Often you will need to set the hook—be alert to gentle tugging on your line. Once you have a fish on, take the reel off of free spool (so there is some drag to slow the fish down) and play it as described earlier.

Floating Boat

It is possible to fish a whitewater river without ever slowing up your downstream progress, except when actually playing and landing a fish. These techniques are especially well suited to fishing from canoes and all the various inflatable craft. There are three basic approaches to floating freely and fishing simultaneously. The first is to cast into the river alongside your boat—if you make sure the water you're tossing a lure or bait into is faster than that your boat is floating in, you can drift fish this way (as described for bank fishing). It's a little tricky figuring out the currents and usually you don't cast upstream like when you're standing on the bank. Also, hanging up on the bottom occurs very frequently.

A second approach, for fishing bait only, requires a deft feel of the bottom—it's another way to bounce the bottom. At the top of a hot spot allow your weight and bait to drop to the bottom. Let the boat drift on downstream, carefully monitoring the weight so that it stays near the bottom yet doesn't get snagged (you should be able to feel it bounce along). You'll find that you will need to raise your rod tip up and down, almost rhythmically, raising it when you sense that the weight is hitting the bottom hard enough that it's going to hang up. People who use this technique tend to use very heavy line and leader so they can pull loose when their rig snags. One autumn I watched two fishermen in a raft pick up six large steelhead on about ten passes down a channel using this technique for bait fishing. At the end of each run they would slide over next to the bank where there wasn't much current, row back upstream, then move out into the channel and make another run.

The last approach to floating and fishing uses a fly or live insects, with or without a casting bubble. If you don't use a bubble, the fly is towed behind on light line. You should pull it well behind the boat, twitching it occasionally. For a little more productive technique, attach the fly to a bubble, as described earlier, and cast it 20 or 30 feet off to the side of the boat. Then let your boat float on downstream alongside of the floating bubble and fly. This technique, since you are fishing on or near the surface, works best in early morning or late evening.

After the Catch

If you land a fish you can delay gutting it for a few hours if you keep it cool and out of direct sunlight. If you are camping, clean your fish and throw the discarded parts into your garbage bag. Don't throw the head, tails and entrails into the river—it's unsightly. If your catch is dinner, fish are very easy to cook. Fry them with a little oil or butter, bake them in foil, or carefully grill them over the campfire. When the flesh pulls apart easily with a fork they are done. If you want a fancier fare, consider dipping them in egg and then in bread crumbs for frying, or including various cut up vegetables inside and alongside when baking.

Commercial fishing trip through Class IV whitewater. (Courtesy of David and Valarie Booth)

Chapter 9

Common Sense and Safety

EACH YEAR THERE ARE SEVERAL DEATHS AND COUNT-less injuries to people challenging our nation's whitewater rivers. Most experts estimate that 90 percent or more of these accidents could have been avoided through attention to issues of safety and just plain old common sense. The ultimate negative outcome of river running is drowning, and somewhere deep down inside of every floater is a fear of that happening. Many people have studied serious river mishaps in detail and have identified four main contributing factors beyond water and natural hazards: Physical injuries, poor physical health or condition, poor swimming skills, and not properly using adequate life jackets. Without a doubt, the last one is the most important—it actually is very difficult to drown with an adequate PFD, properly worn. A local county Deputy Sheriff recently stated that you can count on one hand the river runners on the Rogue River in the last 20 years who have died from drowning while wearing a life jacket! That is a remarkable statistic considering that the Wild and Scenic Rogue is one of the most popular Class IV runs in the United States.

The Boatman

There are two basic rules for river runners to always keep in mind to ensure safety for themselves and their passengers. The first is never extend yourself or your craft beyond capability. Many problems occur because the boatman did not have enough skill or knowledge, and therefore was not up to the challenge. Although literally thousands of floaters each year get into water way beyond their abilities, most will make it through with little or no problem; however, a significant number will not. Rivers are remarkably forgiving; but why entrust your life and limb to luck? I know of a local man who last spring was taken on a 12 mile, Class II float and loved it. A week later he purchased a used raft, frame and oars and rowed the same stretch himself. He remarked how "easy" and how exciting he found whitewater floating. Two weeks later he set out on a three-day,

113

Floating Whitewater Rivers

Class IV stretch of the river. That first morning he fell out of his boat rounding a turn in big waves. That afternoon, in another rapid he missed an entry, hit a rock, went sideways through a hole and capsized. With an unsnapped, unzippered life jacket hooked on one arm, he was pinned under the boat for a while and bounced off of numerous rocks in fast water. The weekend after he arrived home, his boat, frame and oars were in our newspaper's classified ads. He's never been on the river since. A beginner boatman should not step directly, with little rowing or paddling time under his belt, from Class I rapids to Class IV's—but many do. Smaller inflatables and canoes should not be taken into Class V and VI rapids—but many are. Sometimes the line between fun and suicide is very thin.

Two canoeists wearing PFD's to ensure safe whitewater floating.
(Courtesy of Beaver Creek Lodge, Klamath River, California)

It's interesting to look at why people run rivers. Consider asking yourself that question. Without a doubt some run them for the wrong reasons, or at least reasons that represent attempts to "prove" things to others. Reasonable motivations for becoming a whitewater boatman include physical exercise, getting away from the city, enjoying friends, experiencing the wilderness, facing and overcoming challenges, a break from day-to-day tedium, increasing your opportunity to catch fish, and so on (all self-directed rather than other-directed reasons). People who run rivers for psychologically unhealthy reasons tend to be greater safety risks on the water. For example, a fair number of male floaters (usually rafters) are caught up in some form of "macho" routine, trying to impress others with their bravado and masculinity. While on an extended rest break on the Klamath River in California, a gruff-talking, tough-looking boatman approached our rafts. His third sentence was, "I, myself, am a Class V rafter." He followed this with an elongated description of his boating skills and accomplishments, and then an assessment of how simple the Klamath was to run—all this umprompted, uninvited. The "Class V Rafter" may resist scouting (and certainly lining or portaging), take on too much too soon, drink too much, not wear his PFD, and so on, all because of an ongoing concern with his image. There is a female counterpart to this macho male, a type I heard a local guide refer to as "She-man." The problems for her are the same as for the similar male type—trying to prove something to others.

Another sometimes dangerous group on the river are those looking for a sunny, floating party—the "Splash and Giggle" set. They typically are extremely naive, blithely unaware generally of the power of a river, and specifically of the water downstream and how to handle a whitewater boat. Usually a key to the party is lots of booze. Day runs near urban areas are famous for drowning or injuring drunks. Alcohol and driving do not mix, and neither do alcohol and floating. Save your drinking for when you are safely in camp or home at the end of the day.

The first basic rule for river runners was never extend yourself or your craft beyond capability. The second fundamental rule is always prepare for the worst. Obviously, you don't need a life jacket if you never come out of your boat—however, "just in case," wear one. Much of the rest of this chapter relates to "just in cases." No one really expects disaster, but in running rivers it can be just around the next bend. Earlier I described an incident where I lost an oar, hit a rock broadside, and had to row through a large hole and the tailwaves that followed with one oar. None of this was planned, and it's the stuff disasters are made of. Relating specifically to prefloat preparation by the boatman, issues of conditioning and education of passengers are presented below.

Approach whitewater river running as a sport. Like any sport you need to learn the facts, abilities, equipment, and so on, to gain the greatest level of satisfaction and skill possible. Keep yourself in good physical condition. In order to ensure strength and endurance in time of crisis, you need to exercise regularly and frequently (swim or jog, use a rowing machine, or whatever). Give particular attention to

Floating Whitewater Rivers

upper body strength. To run rivers it's not necessary to have a Herculean build (for kayaking that could be a distinct disadvantage). For most whitewater, the average 12-year-old can handle it (except in very large boats) if they make no mistakes. But humans make errors—to increase your chance of "powering" a boat out of trouble or swimming to safety when dumped, keep in good shape!

When you're preparing for the worst, if you are carrying passengers don't forget to prepare them. If you go down, chance are good you'll take them with you. Make certain they know what to do in an emergency. Be especially clear about hanging on in the rapids, the notion of "high side" when the boat begins tipping (against a rock, sideways through a hole, and so on), and what to do if thrown into the water.

Always be prepared for the possibility of a river mishap.

Safety Equipment

Begin your safety check for a river run by looking over your boat, paddles or oars, frame, and everything else to be floated. The last thing any boatman wants is equipment failure in the middle of a rapid—you can decrease the possibility of a problem ranging from inconvenience to tragedy by making sure everything is in good shape. For inflatables, make sure there are no tears or leaks and that the air pressure is where it belongs (see the manufacturer's recommendations); for hard boats make sure they are free of cracks, splitting seams, rot in wood, loose braces or float bags, and the like. For all craft, be aware of the weight capacity and don't overload them. Check your oars and oarlocks or paddle(s) carefully. Raft frames need to be strong, crack-free, and with no sharp corners or edges. And if you're carrying gear, it should be safely secured with no ropes or straps that can entangle the floaters in time of trouble.

Personal Flotation Device (PFD)

As stated earlier, the life jacket is the single-most important piece of equipment for whitewater river runners. A fundamental fact about PFD's is that they are of little use laying in the bottom of the boat. Even with a life jacket on, and all snapped up, a swim through big whitewater can be tough—without it, the holes, rocks, currents and waves can make it impossible.

The U. S. Coast Guard sorts all PFD's into five classes. Each has a "buoyancy rating"—you need minimally one pound of buoyancy to each 10 pounds of body weight. I personally feel more comfortable using jackets well above that minimum. A Type I PFD (often called a Mae West) has traditionally been filled with kapok in plastic bags. These jackets provide good buoyancy (22 pounds), but if the plastic bags are punctured they become dangerous. Most modern jackets of all types are filled with closed-cell foam, eliminating the need to keep water away from the material that provides the buoyancy. Type I's will float a conscious or unconscious person to a vertical position, head above the water. A common complaint with these jackets is that they are uncomfortable for extended wearing or for any small boat paddling.

The common Type II PFD, shaped like an upside down letter "U," is unsuitable for whitewater use. It was designed for lakes, for calm flatwater. The Type II is never used by commercial outfitters, except occasionally on Class I rivers. The most commonly used life jacket for whitewater is the Type III, available in several different styles and sizes and colors. It usually has 15½ pounds of buoyancy, although there are models being marketed up to nearly double that. It completely encircles the wearer, like a puffy sleeveless jacket, yet is comfortable to wear even for paddlers of small boats. By varying the amount of buoyant filling front and back, it is designed to keep a conscious swimmer in a vertical position.

Type IV PFD's are limited to ring buoys ("lifeguard rings") and floating seat cushions. Although they may meet your local regulations that require you carry PFD's, they are unsuitable for whitewater use. Several types of jackets comprise the Type V category. Some varieties are made specifically for whitewater rafting and very popular with commercial outfitters. They have 22 pounds or more of buoyancy and will keep a conscious swimmer in a vertical position. However, they tend to be somewhat uncomfortable for extended use, especially for paddlers of small boats.

Two PFD Types

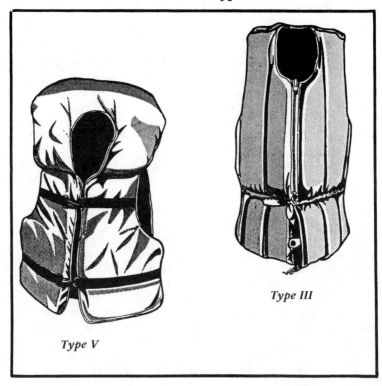

Type III

Type V

Boat Repair Kit

Some mishaps in river running will do damage to your boat. You can incur additional risk if you continue running without repairing it. Some things often can be replaced more easily than repaired, like paddles or oars, oarlocks, D-rings, straps, and valves. For extended trips, carry extra of these items (see the River Trip Checklist, Repair Items, Chapter VII).

Boaters in inflatable craft need to carry a *patch kit*. The most common damage they will face is holes or rips in an air chamber. If you can't fix it, by lining or portaging rapids, you probably can float to your take-out (on whatever air chambers remain intact). However, it is dangerous sometimes to try. A patch kit typically has pieces of the material your inflatable is made of (different weights if the floor is heavier) and the appropriate adhesive. In addition you may carry methyl ethyl ketone (MEK, for PVC) or toluol (for synthetic rubber coated materials) or fine sandpaper to prepare the boat and patch surfaces to be joined, scissors, brush for the glue, rag, and a heavy needle and thread for long tears.

Assortment of items for making repairs on boat, accessories, and gear.

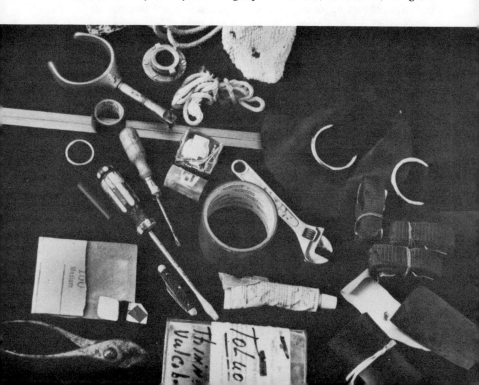

For all boatmen, whatever their craft size and structural material, the all-purpose repair item is good quality *duct tape*. You can fix all kinds of problems with it, from pinhole leaks to cracked paddle blades to ripped life jackets. Rafters using frames should also consider bringing tools for any nuts, bolts, and so on (and extra of the hardware), bailing wire, and epoxy. Floaters in fiberglass or plastic boats can carry a repair kit suited to the material their boat is made of (for example, fiberglass cloth, resin and catalyst), although minor repairs on the river are usually done with duct tape. Aluminum canoes and drift boats can use epoxy made for that metal for very minor seam cracks or tears. Again, on the river it's often most efficient just to use duct tape. You would be amazed how resourceful people are when faced with equipment problems in wilderness areas. Always bring a small container full of repair items and barring major disaster to your boat or gear, your float will be completed as planned.

Health and First Aid

As part of the preparation for any river trip you'll need a number of ordinary health care items as well as an emergency first aid kit. For a short float, the health care supplies may just be a bottle of suntan oil, sun blocking lotion, some toilet paper, or a pair of sunglasses with a safety strap. For multi-day trips, common additions are lip balm (for chapping), lotion, prescribed medications, insect repellent, vitamin and mineral supplements, biodegradable soap, sanitary napkins or tampons, toothbrush, toothpaste, razor, and a comb. My eyesight is sufficiently poor that I always carry a backup pair of glasses in case I lose my regular ones. Unless you absolutely can't do without, do not carry or use various forms of fragrance (deodorants, perfumes, after-shave lotions, and so on)—on summer runs, every time you swim they end up in the river.

Give some serious thought to your emergency *first aid kit:* There is the possibility that it will be called upon to save someone's life. First, if you don't already know, learn basic first aid procedures (including artificial respiration and some CPR). There are various books on the subject, or better yet, take Red Cross sponsored or other comprehensive first aid classes. You need to know what to do if someone burns themselves on the stove or takes in too much water during an unplanned swim or cuts their thumb while making dinner or breaks an arm in a fall. Once you learn standard first aid procedures you are in a good position to put together a functional and comprehensive emergency kit. Mine includes bandages and compresses of varying sizes (and gauze and adhesive tape to make what they don't cover), various ointments, salves and lotions (for disinfecting, eliminating itching and pain, or preventing infection), ace bandage (for sprains and strains), mini-flashlight, tweezers, nail clippers, scissors, and an assortment of tablets and capsules, both prescription and nonprescription. The over-the-counter drugs are for headaches (and other aches and pains), upset stomach, and upper and lower respiratory discomfort (stuffy nose, cough, and so on). If you wish to carry prescription drugs, explain their purpose to your family physician and most will prescribe some for you in very small quantities. However, if you carry these more potent and potentially dangerous drugs, be extremely clear as to dosage, side effects, and drug interactions. I carry medication in the form of tablets or suppositories for pain, emotional distress, diarrhea, and nausea or vomiting.

Another item in my first aid kit is a snakebite kit. There's a lot of controversy among medical professionals regarding whether lay people should use them. Many victims have had more problems with the infection created by attempts to extract venom than with the venom itself. If a doctor is only an hour or two away and the snake is only a small Western Rattlesnake, I would avoid using the kit. I would suggest you consult with your local physician regarding his views on snakebite kits.

Other Safety Gear

There are other forms of safety devices not yet covered in this chapter. A must for hard-shell kayakers and not a bad idea for other floaters facing big rapids is the whitewater *helmet*. Kayakers sometimes find themselves floating upside down in rocky, fast water and a good helmet can prevent something between a bruise and death if they contact underwater boulders. The helmet should protect the sides of the head as well as front, back and top, and be well-lined with at least 1/2 inch of quality foam padding. Some helmets made for other sports (like football or motorcycling) will work in a pinch, but the best and safest are made specifically for whitewater river running.

Probably the most common kind of safety gear not yet covered is *rope*. Lengths of rope are used for various lashing requirements as well as being central in rescue operations and lining procedures. Generally, bright colored, floating, low stretch rope made from synthetic materials works the best for river running applications. Ropes are used to unwrap rafts and right capsized craft, tied to boats for bow, stern and lifelines, and coiled up and thrown as rescue lines to floating or otherwise endangered river runners. Tossing a rope a long distance accurately is a lot harder than it may look. There are available commercially-made "throw bags" where the rope is coiled inside the bag—these are relatively easy to use, even by someone who has never tried one before. As mentioned previously, ropes can be dangerous. Never tie one to anybody, not the rescuer or the rescuee (the one possible exception to this rule is noted later). Always be certain that they cannot entangle anybody. In situations where abrasion or strain or dislocation is likely from severe pull, wear gloves and wrap the rope one turn around a tree or a boulder or something else secure. This is called belaying and it eliminates a direct pull on the person holding the rope. In a pinch you can sit down facing the direction

Kayaker wearing protective helmet to prevent head injuries. (Courtesy of Scott Pitts)

the rope comes from, pass the end around your life jacketed back, and then holding on firmly with both hands (one on the incoming line, the other on the tail of the rope after it comes around your body), use your body to belay. Be certain not to get entangled in the loose end should you be overwhelmed and have to let go. Finally, there is some controversy about how (and if) you throw a line to someone who has been dumped into whitewater. Look over the situation carefully and be certain that by setting a line out and pulling them toward you they will experience less trauma than if they simply continue to float unassisted to the bottom of the rapid. You potentially could drag them into worse hazards than they otherwise will face where they are.

Heat and Cold

Generally less of a problem than cold, nonetheless floaters should be aware of potential problems from *overheating*. Everyone is aware of sunburn because it is visible and painful. Be alert to skin reddening and burning and use protective lotions or cover up with clothing when necessary. People are generally less aware of the other kinds of body reactions to a lot of sun or heat. Most floaters deal with ordinary overheating by removing some clothes, jumping in the river, and taking in a lot of fluids. The three conditions created by heat are heat stroke, heat exhaustion, and heat cramps. These reactions all occur when the body cannot eliminate excess heat are are more likely to occur when large amounts of water and/or salt are lost through heavy sweating during and after strenuous exercise.

With heat stroke the body temperature may go as high as 106 degrees and the skin will look hot, dry and red—the sweating mechanism is blocked and the pulse is rapid. I've never encountered this condition on the river, but it can be fatal. Immediately begin a process of cooling with river water, but watch for over-chilling. More common on the river, on long hot days, is heat exhaustion (fatigue and weakness due primarily to dehydration) and heat cramps (muscular pains and spasms primarily due to salt loss)—sometimes these two reactions occur together, and in both cases, body temperature will be normal. If you are sweating a lot, be certain to take in plenty of water and a little salt. A first aid remedy for heat exhaustion and heat cramps is sips of salt water (1/2 teaspoon of salt in a half glass of water) every 10 or 15 minutes for about an hour. Supplement this with externally applied cool river water. In the rare instance where the victim of advanced heat exhaustion vomits, you'll need to get him to a hospital for intravenous salt solution. Don't let yourself or your fellow floaters get into this serious a condition. Watch for overheating.

More often a problem for whitewater river runners than reactions to heat is the body's reaction to cold, a condition called *hypothermia*. The first time you pull someone into your boat who has only been in the water a few minutes and find them weak and disoriented, you'll gain a healthy respect for the effects of cold. For those of you who float during the winter and early spring, you need to be especially alert—those times of year, on most rivers, both the air and the water will be cold. Hypothermia is an insidious disorder in that the victim generally does not recognize how seriously his body is reacting to cold. As the body's core temperature is lowering there are stages of reaction, one blurring into the next. It starts with intense shivering and fatigue, moving to numbness, thickness of speech, disorientation and drowsiness, and finishes with irrationality, decreased pulse rate, unconsciousness and death. Sitting in a boat, poorly dressed, on a cold day, this process will be subtle and slow, but hopefully recognized early by fellow boaters. However, if you get tossed into the river, it can occur much more rapidly than most people realize. An added problem is that a sudden dunk in very cold water (45 degrees or less) also can cause an immediate breathing problem where the reaction is one of gasping and rapid respiration, leading to hyperventilation and panic. In just 3 or 4 minutes a swimmer may be too fatigues or confused or emotionally distraught to assist in his own progress to safety.

The best cure for hypothermia is good prevention. In chilly weather on cold rivers wet suits (or dry suits with warm layers underneath, see Chapter VII) are an absolute must. They will prevent the tremendous heat loss created by wet clothing or direct contact with the river when dunked. Only on moderately cold weather trips, where the river is also not very cold, can you safely wear rain gear over wool as described earlier. Another form of prevention besides adequate clothing is constant vigilance for the signs of lowering body temperature—the sooner it's recognized, the easier it is to deal with. The first thing you might recognize in yourself or fellow floaters is shivering; that will be followed by weakness and/or speech and body actions that appear similar to that of being drunk. Finally, fatigue seems to be associated with more susceptibility to hypothermia. Avoid getting extremely tired.

When you spot the initial minor symptoms of hypothermia, get over to the shore immediately and warm up (clothes, hot drinks, build a fire or start your stove, and so on). However, if the symptoms are more than minor you'll need heat from an external source-because the victim's body has lost the ability to regain normal temperature (regardless of the type or amount of clothes you put on him). If a house or motel or whatever is available, fill a bathtub with warm water (about 110 degrees) and put him in it. In more wilderness situations, you can strip the victim and yourself and get both of you (and another stripped person, if possible) into a sleeping bag. Effectively, your warm body and the warming air inside the bag provide external heat for the hypothermia victim, slowly allowing his body temperature to rise back up to normal. You should carefully monitor the victim's breathing and be prepared to administer first aid (artificial respiration at one-half the normal rate) if necessary. Your first aid training (as suggested earlier) should include a detailed look at hypothermia, its course, prevention, and treatment. Probably the golden rule of treatment is the more immediately it is administered the better the results.

It may look clear, but unfortunately the water in most rivers is not safe to drink.

Water Purification

River runners may face a health hazard if they plan to drink the water found in streams and rivers during their trip. In fact, the most common health problem seen on long wilderness trips is stomach and intestinal discomfort, and this can be caused by drinking bad water. The surest approach to safe water is to bring it from home. My coolers are kept cold by one gallon plastic milk containers filled with tap water and frozen. As the ice slowly melts, I have drinking water. I can speed up the melt if I desire by setting a container out into the sun or for emergencies, toss a chunk of ice into a pan on the stove.

Unless you know for certain to the contrary, presume all the water in the wilderness is unsafe to drink. There are various approaches to purifying water, but always start with the clearest, cleanest-looking, flowing water you can find (most often from an incoming creek). You can boil it for three to five minutes, then pour it back and forth between two containers to aerate it. The three most common approaches to purification by chemicals use halazone tablets, ordinary household chlorine bleach, or an iodine solution. The simplest of these is to put ten or eleven drops of chlorine bleach in a gallon of cold water, mix very gently but thoroughly, then let stand for 30 to 45 minutes. During this waiting time disinfection is completed and the chlorine will dissipate as a gas into the air. Finally, there are very efficient commercial filter systems designed for purification of drinking water. Most are very fast and effective, but some are also quite expensive.

River Mishaps

As the final topic for this chapter on safety, a variety of problems specific to whitewater river running will be discussed. If you find yourself in one of these predicaments, you need to be able to quickly and efficiently get yourself out of trouble.

Unplanned Swims

If you spend a lot of time on rivers, sooner or later you are going to find yourself separated from the seat in your boat and pitched into the water. I recommend that every floater, as part of training, purposely jump into little rapids and float them in a PFD. Float on your back with your feet together and forward to fend off hazards. Use your arms like oars to gain a little control as to your direction. If you try this you'll find that by relaxing and not fighting the river, typically you'll float through even rocky rapids pretty easily. Near the bottom of the rapid, when you're sure you are out of the worst of it, turn over onto your stomach, point sideways and a little upstream (a forward ferry), and swim for shore.

Once you've practiced "body surfing" you need to be aware of some details that can be extremely important in big rapids. If possible, hang onto your boat (except those without flotation), but be careful to stay alongside or upstream of it. If you are hanging onto the downstream side you risk being pinned in the middle of boat-rock sandwich. Also, do not allow your feet to be forced into narrow crevices or spaces between rocks or other hazards where you might get trapped. If the water is very turbulent, like going through holes, breathe through your mouth with your lips open but teeth clenched to avoid taking in a lot of water. You should be aware that holes will sometimes hold a swimmer for a while. In very large holes, some experts suggest that you may have to literally dive down to catch the downstream current. Basically, you are trying to follow the hydraulics of the hole; time the dive as you crest the reversal and feel the current forcing you down. Finally, in long or very rough rapids you may not want to wait until the end of them to get to safety. Just like in boating, eddies are a place of haven, to rest or scurry up onto a rock or the shore.

Two floaters in the water, body surfing behind their boat.

Capsized Boats

For hard-shell kayakers, capsizing is generally part of big water floating and they deal with it by rolling back up (or bailing out if that doesn't work). For other craft, especially the large ones, capsizing can be a crisis. If flipping over is inevitable and cannot be prevented by moving to the high side, make a safe exit from your boat. Don't allow a raft frame, or oars, or drift boat gunwales, or whatever, to hit you. Be certain you get free from possible entanglement or falling into the water underneath your boat. Sometimes you can make a big leap to get clear of everything. Don't worry about anyone else or gear or the boat—take care of yourself as described in the section on unplanned swims. Once into slow water or onto the bank, if there are others in the flip, make sure they each took care of themselves, then concern yourself with your boat and gear. For large rafts you can tie lines on one side and stand on the other and fall back into the water to flip the boat back upright. Find a place with low or no current because this can be more difficult than it sounds. You may have to unload all the gear out of an upside down boat to do it.

Hung-up Boats

Sometimes just an annoyance, other times a life-threatening crisis, occasionally all kinds of whitewater craft are susceptible to getting stopped in midstream. The worst form of this problem is wrapping, a condition generally reserved for inflatables (discussed in the next section). The most common form of hang-up is running up onto a rock or shallows. If you are on a rock in heavy water, try all kinds of weight shifting, rocking the boat, and prying with your paddles or oars before you get out of the boat to try pushing and tugging. It may also be possible to get a line to someone on shore who with a little ingenuity can pull you free. On one occasion I floated past a raft hung-up at the base of a rapid and tossed them a line and the momentum of my boat pulled them loose. With any use of ropes be certain not to entangle anyone. Running aground in shallows generally is less a problem simply because very shallow water is not so dangerous. Get out of the boat and push and pull until you reach deeper water. Be certain that the boat is properly oriented and you quickly get back to your seat if the shallows dumps into big water obstacles.

Hard boats and sometimes inflatables will wash up against a rock or a steep bank and be held there without technically "wrapping;" this is called *broaching*. This occurs in fast water where the current has a lot of force. The biggest problem you face in this situation is swamping or crushing (of hard boats). Immediately, in all boats move to the downstream side—if the upstream side dives under the water inflatables will likely wrap. Hard-shell kayakers can't move like in a raft, but should lean into the rock to prevent the current from impacting directly on the deck of their boat. Avoid tipping upstream in all craft! You may be able to push yourself free (start a pivot around a rock) with your hands or paddle or oar. In large craft it may help to rock and bounce or move passengers (and other weight) to the part of the boat that is farthest out in safe current. The same thing is accomplished if a person holds onto a line and jumps out into fast water. As a last resort, you may have to get a line to shore to free a broached boat.

Wrapped Inflatables

The most common crisis for large inflatables is wrapping. In wrapping, a boat is first broached on a rock, then the current pushes the upstream tube under the water. Now the entire floor surface is at

Freeing a Wrapped Raft

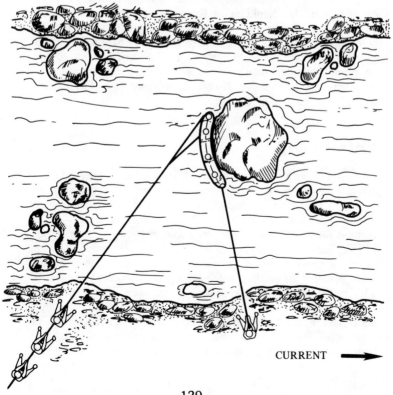

CURRENT ➝

the mercy of the force of the river. It will wrap the boat tightly around the rock until it is seriously pinned. It can take most of a day and some cutting of the raft material to free it. As stated before, many a wrap is prevented by immediate shift of weight to the downstream side of your boat. This prevents the upstream side of your craft from plunging down into the water and letting the current play against the floor.

If a wrap occurs, you will either have to scramble up onto the exposed high tube or the wrap rock itself, or jump into the river and float out of trouble. Once wrapped, barring significant water level drop or amazing good luck, you'll have to pull the raft free using lines from shore. Typically, one end of the raft is secured to a hauling line. You can tie to several D-rings, part of the frame, a thwart, or by cutting a small hole in the floor, the front or back tube. Several tie-on points decrease the chance of ripping things loose. If you have access to a winch it will make the job easier. Sometimes it helps to deflate part of the boat. Depending on the shoreline, it may be difficult to get a good angle of pull. If all else fails, try slitting or cutting out a portion of the floor, or all of it if necessary.

Last summer I sat near our campsite watching a rescue in the middle of Blossom Bar Rapid on the Rogue River. It was orchestrated by a county Sheriff crew who reportedly had unwrapped dozens of boats from the far right rock of the Picket Fence (see Chapter V). It took two winches, cutting the floor, about two hours of rescuing all the people and gear, and then a lot of grunting and groaning to finally get a ten-man raft to shore. No matter how you look at it, it's a tough, time-consuming job.

Entrapment

As stated earlier, the number one fear of most experienced river runners is entrapment. Entrapment means you are pinned in an immediately life-threatening situation. A couple of years ago a kayaker, out of his boat, got a leg wedged between two below-the-surface rocks at Blossom Bar—his head was a foot under the surface. Long after he drowned, his body was winched out of the rapids. This kind of entrapment can also occur to someone just standing in swift current. If your foot becomes stuck and the river topples you over, even a life jacket may not keep your head above water. The attempts at rescue for rock-wedged floaters is first to try to get their head above water, and second to pull them loose. Another common hazard for swimmers is downed trees. They may act as strainers, allowing the river to flow through, but not you. You have two options as you approach a strainer and usually only a second or two to decide which to take. Either don't grab anything and keep your momentum going (and hopefully you'll wash on through) or grab for the highest branch you can reach and try to pull yourself up and out of the current. To rescue someone from a downed tree you should follow the same two steps as described for persons wedged between rocks. In both situations you may have to violate the fundamental rule "never tie a rope on any person" to keep someone's head above water.

It is possible to get entrapped in your boat, where you and your craft are together forced under the water. If your kayak is crushed on top of you or your inflatable wraps around you, the situation is even more lethal than the entrapment of a swimmer. Whistling Bird, a rapid mentioned earlier (on the Owyhee River in Oregon), has a massive slab that has slid into the river. Its lower surface angles down into the river with strong current flowing under it. If you were swept under the slab, after about 15 feet you and your boat would be forced under water and pinned there. Always be on the lookout for undercut banks and boulders, for they can have the same effect. If you are in your craft and nearing a wrap or underwater pin or a strainer, consider getting out of your boat and into the water. This requires a quick judgment call, one dependent upon all the characteristics of the problem. It's better to be swimming free in a big rapid, for example, than having a 16-foot raft pin you to a rock. If you are involved in a rescue of an entrapped boat and its occupant(s), consider cutting up the craft and/or using ropes to pull it free, again dependent upon the specific situation.

General Guidelines

When dealing with river mishaps, a lot of quick thinking and sometimes creative work is required. Above all, attend to people! In time of crisis, who really cares about river bags and paddles—it's only money. As stated earlier, your first thought when you get in trouble should be to get yourself safely to shore. Once you accomplish that, your second thought should be what kind of assistance you can offer others. Once all the people are attended to and safe, then you can concern yourself about boats and gear.

Chapter 10 _____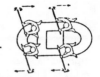

Our Whitewater Rivers

A COUPLE OF HUNDRED YEARS AGO OUR ANCESTORS, and before that the American Indians, took a lot of things for granted—like clean air, open spaces, tall forests, and free-flowing rivers. With population expansion, growing commercialism, and high technology over these two centuries our nation finds itself in something of a dilemma. We no longer can take rivers for granted. Dams, diversions and other developments, and pollution change the waterways and the landscape that were untouched for thousands of years.

Rivers provide pleasure—recreation, relaxation, excitement, exercise, nature study, and so on—they are one of America's most precious resources, something beautiful, something to be protected, to be saved. In 1968 Congress recognized a need to enact some regulation of industrial and population impact on our rivers. They established the National Wild and Scenic Rivers Systems (Public Law 90-542) and designated segments of eight rivers, totaling less than 1000 miles, to be protected. At the time of this writing the total number of rivers with protected sections (both Federal and State designation) has grown to over 300, the total mileage now over 18,000 miles. This may sound like a lot to those of you new to this issue, but consider the fact that there are well over three million miles of river in this country!

Whitewater boating is really a combination of many and varied pleasurable factors. For most, the two at the top of the list are rapids and relatively undisturbed environment. Sometimes it's fun to float through populated areas, but far and away most of us find the greatest pleasure in wilderness waterways. The National Wild and Scenic Rivers designations, where it's not too late, not only prevent the drowning of rivers by reservoirs behind dams and the fouling of rivers by pollutants, but assures minimal additional human encroachment in the nearby landscape. It is important that we continue to evaluate and expand the river mileage in the system to ensure that we and those in generations to come can enjoy our nation's rivers. There are a number of groups of people concerned about river preservation. One such group is the American Rivers Conservation Council.

Based in Washington, D. C., ARCC is a national organization dedicated exclusively to the conservation of our nation's rivers. They provide an ongoing lobbying voice in Congress, work with all the various Federal agencies like the Forest Service and Department of Interior, and mobilize resistance when plans are made to destroy wild rivers. For up-to-date river status from all around the country they serve as the clearing house source (for information: ARCC, 322 Fourth Street, N. E., Washington, D. C. 20002).

Wild and scenic whitewater.

River Descriptions

The purpose of this last chapter is to identify and briefly describe a large number of rivers. It is not intended to substitute for a guidebook for any of them. For virtually every river run listed below, there are excellent guidebooks available, books which explain in great detail the information I have skimmed over lightly. Many also add specific descriptions of major rapids with step-by-step instructions on how to safely run them. The sanest approach to any first-time run is to talk to people that have run it (preferably run it a lot), study guidebooks, then when on the water stop and scout any rapid that you think you might have difficulty with. Ultimately, you are responsible for your own well-being. Neither I nor the publisher assume any responsibility for people using this book to learn how to float whitewater or to select particular runs to attempt. Your good judgment and common sense are essential to ensure your safety.

The descriptions I provide below only in small part come from personal experience. I wish I could say I have run the 100-plus stretches of river listed, but time and miles keep getting in my way. For rivers I have not run I have gleaned information from an immense stack of books and magazines (see references). I hope, especially in those cases where two sources contradicted one another, that I have not made any glaringly incorrect statements. I have two levels of description in this chapter. The majority of them are extended and cover several specific points (like distance and some of the best rapids). The remainder are just teasers to spark enough interest to send you looking for more information.

The extended descriptions begin with the general *location*, the state and what portion of that state. The second entry is the specific *run*, that is, the put-in and the take-out. Some rivers are presented more than once because they have more than one popular run. Third is the approximate *distance*, in river miles. Bear in mind that the vehicle miles, the shuttle, may be considerably longer for some rivers. The fourth entry is the *time* of year generally best for floating that stretch, and fifth is an overall *difficulty* rating (eliminating any rapids that are usually lined or portaged). Any consideration of time year and difficulty must take into account the water level. If a Class II river is flooding, and that river becomes unrunnable at high water, my time of year and difficulty rating become irrelevant. As discussed earlier, when a river's flow increases or decreases (sometimes just a little), it may be like running a whole different river, and not necessarily in predictable ways to a novice. Some rapids as the water rises may wash out or become high speed death traps; some, as the water level drops, may turn into mere riffles or end up an impassable rock garden. You can usually get details on water flow effects on a run from guidebooks or whitewater folks who are very familiar with that particular river. My time of year description relates the months in which there usually is the "right" amount of water to float that stretch. The difficulty rating reflects what level of skill a boatman should have to attempt a run at that time of year, which is generally when most people would be on the water. The five levels used for these ratings are practice, novice, intermediate, advanced, and expert. For some craft, like open canoes, you should adjust all the ratings up a step.

The next entry in the extended descriptions is the feature *rapids.* For most of us, prior to, during, and after a run, we are focused on a few spots in the river. Our memories and stories for years will continue to keep a few select rapids alive from each river run. For each description I have chosen the three rapids I think most likely will haunt you before and stay with you afterwards, giving a typical rating of difficulty (class in parentheses) to each. Entry seven in the description is a brief phrase to describe the *environment,* a teaser to at least let you know whether you are camping on sagebrush, canyon boulders, or in a tree-lined grassy meadow. Finally, each description is completed with some *comments* to add bits and pieces of information to the seven-step outline above.

In order to organize the presentation of over 100 runs scattered all over the contiguous 48 states (I've not included Alaska since it is inaccessible to the majority of river runners), I've arbitrarily divided the nation into four sections: East Coast (all of the coastal states plus a few others very close); East Central (from the eastern coastal states over to and including Minnesota to Louisiana); West Central (the rest of the U. S. except the Western Coastal States); and West Coast (Washington, Oregon and California). My listings of rivers are not exhaustive and are nowhere near covering all of the whitewater sections of rivers in this country. However, I have tried to include the majority of the popular ones, the talked about ones, the runs that you may want to consider making your next float trip.

There is nothing quite so beautiful or so awesome as boiling, tumbling whitewater.

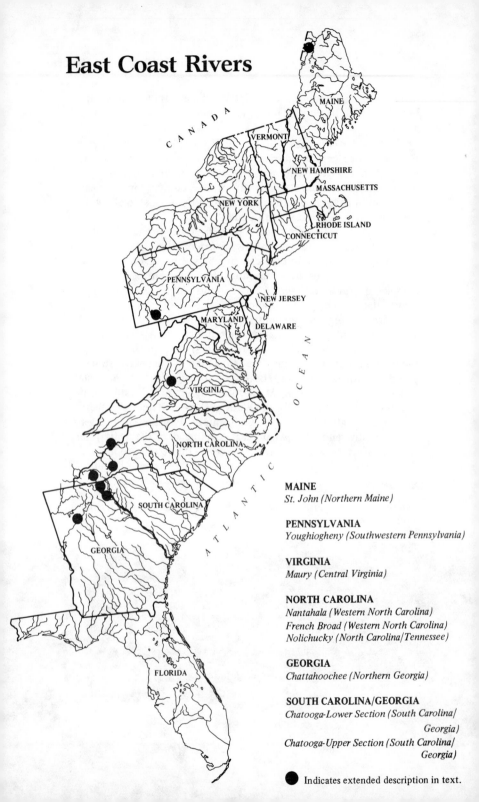

East Coast Rivers

MAINE
NEW HAMPSHIRE
VERMONT
MASSACHUSETTS
NEW YORK
RHODE ISLAND
CONNECTICUT
PENNSYLVANIA
NEW JERSEY
MARYLAND
DELAWARE
VIRGINIA
NORTH CAROLINA
SOUTH CAROLINA
GEORGIA
FLORIDA

CANADA

ATLANTIC OCEAN

MAINE
St. John (Northern Maine)

PENNSYLVANIA
Youghiogheny (Southwestern Pennsylvania)

VIRGINIA
Maury (Central Virginia)

NORTH CAROLINA
Nantahala (Western North Carolina)
French Broad (Western North Carolina)
Nolichucky (North Carolina/Tennessee)

GEORGIA
Chattahoochee (Northern Georgia)

SOUTH CAROLINA/GEORGIA
Chatooga-Lower Section (South Carolina/
                                    Georgia)
Chatooga-Upper Section (South Carolina/
                                    Georgia)

● Indicates extended description in text.

RIVER: *Chattahoochee*
LOCATION: Northern Georgia
RUN: Highway 255 Bridge to Arn Bridge
DISTANCE: 10 miles
TIME: All year
DIFFICULTY: Novice/Intermediate
RAPIDS: Buck Island (II), Three Ledges (II+), Horseshoe (II+)
ENVIRONMENT: Sparsely populated rolling hills
COMMENTS: Much of land along the river is privately owned and some of it is posted. There's a county park halfway on the run if you want a shorter trip. After the confluence of the Chattahoochee and the Soquee, for the last mile and one-half, this is a flatwater float.

RIVER: *Chatooga (Lower Section)*
LOCATION: South Carolina/Georgia
RUN: U. S. Highway 76 Bridge to Tugaloo Lake
DISTANCE: 10 miles
TIME: All year
DIFFICULTY: Expert
RAPIDS: Woodall Shoals (V+), Sock'm-Dog (V), Corkscrew (IV)
ENVIRONMENT: Forested mountain area
COMMENTS: This stretch ("Section 4") of the Chatooga is extremely tough going, for experts only, and at high water levels (above 2.0 feet) gets tougher. Like Section 3, the landscape is magnificent, the foliage lush. The river is designated Wild and Scenic and float trip registration is mandatory. This Section can be combined with Section 3 upstream for about as exciting a 22-mile float as you'll find anywhere.

RIVER: *Chatooga (Upper Section)*
LOCATION: South Carolina/Georgia
RUN: Earl's Ford to U. S. Highway 76 Bridge
DISTANCE: 12 miles
TIME: All year
DIFFICULTY: Advanced
RAPIDS: Narrows (IV), Painted Rock (IV), Bull Sluice (V)
ENVIRONMENT: Forested mountain area
COMMENTS: The Chatooga flows through the Great Smoky Mountains; the scenery is great and wildlife is frequently seen. This section of the Chatooga ("Section 3") was featured in the film *Deliverance* and is for experts only. The river is designated Wild and Scenic and float trip registration is mandatory. Above Earl's Ford, Sections 1 and 2, are much milder and good for novices.

RIVER: *French Broad*
LOCATION: Western North Carolina
RUN: Barnard to U. S. 25/70
DISTANCE: 8 miles
TIME: April to October
DIFFICULTY: Intermediate
RAPIDS: Big Pillow (III+), Needle Rock (II+), Frank Bell (III+)
ENVIRONMENT: Sparsely populated rolling hills
COMMENTS: The French Broad is basically a drop and pool river with a number of rapids of moderate difficulty. The railroad tracks are alongside for most of this run. For a couple of months of the year you can put-in on Big Laurel Creek (Bridge at Highway 25/70 and 208) for a trip through a narrow gorge and some Class IV action. If you float Big Laurel, it joins French Broad a little over three miles upstream of the take-out.

RIVER: *Maury*
LOCATION: Central Virginia
RUN: Calfpasture/Little Calfpasture to Rockbridge Baths
DISTANCE: 6 miles
TIME: February to June
DIFFICULTY: Advanced
RAPIDS: Devil's Kitchen (IV), Corner (IV), Indian Pool (III)
ENVIRONMENT: Sparsely populated mountain pass
COMMENTS: This float is through Goshen Pass in the Blue Ridge Mountains. Rock canyons with trees and flowering shrubs, and homes/cabins are seen from the river. Be careful not to offend the landowners of private property. Route 39 follows the river for this run, making it convenient if you want to run it twice in one day. This stretch is short in miles, but has plenty of technical action.

RIVER: *Nantahala*
LOCATION: Western North Carolina
RUN: Powerhouse Bridge to Wesser Falls
DISTANCE: 8 miles
TIME: April to October
DIFFICULTY: Intermediate
RAPIDS: Patton's Run (III+), Quarry (II), Nantahala Falls (III+)
ENVIRONMENT: Deep gorge with lush vegetation
COMMENTS: Certainly not a wilderness river, but it is beautiful nonetheless. Nantahala gorge is 1000 feet deep and lined with laurels, rhododendron, and other mountain trees and shrubs. The take-out is at the store/restaurant above Wesser Falls, an honest

138

Class VI series of jagged ledges (it is only rarely attempted). The first half of this run has nearly non-stop whitewater.

RIVER: *Nolichucky*
LOCATION: North Carolina/Tennessee
RUN: Poplar to Unaka Springs
DISTANCE: 9 miles
TIME: April to September
DIFFICULTY: Intermediate/Advanced
RAPIDS: Railroad Bridge (III+), Quartermile (IV), Roostertail (III)
ENVIRONMENT: Heavily forested deep canyon
COMMENTS: The Nolichucky Canyon is well over 2000 feet deep in some places, providing floaters with a spectacular landscape as they wind through the Cherokee National Forest. There are several Class · III or above rapids, but the river becomes too dangerous to run when the water level exceeds 3 feet. At the state line (a little over half way) hike up the trail at Devil's Creek to the beautiful waterfall.

RIVER: *St. John*
LOCATION: Northern Maine
RUN: Red Pine Camp to Allagash Village
DISTANCE: 83 miles
TIME: April to June
DIFFICULTY: Intermediate
RAPIDS: Big Black (III), Big (III), many minor rapids
ENVIRONMENT: Forestland
COMMENTS: The St. John flows through wild country, a magnificent journey through the forest wilderness of Maine. You are very much on your own for this float. To reach the put-in you'll need to get a permit to travel private road (from the International Paper Company). Areas for campsites on this river are designated and some of them require fire permits.

RIVER: *Youghiogheny*
LOCATION: Southwestern Pennsylvania
RUN: Ohiopyle to Bruner Run
DISTANCE: 7 miles
TIME: April to October
DIFFICULTY: Advanced
RAPIDS: Entrance (IV), Cucumber (IV), River's End (IV)
ENVIRONMENT: Forested highlands
COMMENTS: The Yough has been described as the most popular river in the East. Some weekends it gets extremely crowded. The put-in is just below Ohiopyle Falls (a dangerous Class VI). At lower

water levels (below 1000 cfs) this river can be run by open canoes; at higher water levels the river becomes very powerful with almost continuous rapids in some areas. The beginning of the run is called the Loop—in this section of a little over a mile the river drops nearly 100 feet. There is a take-out at the end of the Loop if you want to shuttle back upstream and do it again.

Other East Coast Rivers

Allagash (Class II, Maine): Various sections of 98 miles of this river are very popular with canoeists. The landscape, except for heavily logged areas, is beautiful and wildlife is abundant.

Dead (Class IV, Maine): The Dead River offers 22 miles of wilderness scenery and lots of whitewater in the run from Long Dam Falls to the Forks. You'll begin with a 6-mile float through marshlands and portage around Grand Falls, then 16 miles of nearly continuous rapids.

Hudson (Class IV, New York): The headwaters of the Hudson offer a fine wilderness float for a brief time each spring (April to June). There are several sections of very sportive, but very cold, whitewater.

James (Class IV, Virginia): This river offers a popular float of 9 miles through a 300-plus acre nature refuge. You'll also pass through the town of Richmond.

Kennebec (Class IV, Maine): This beautiful river passes through primitive wilderness areas (near Moosehead Lake). It can usually be run from May through September.

Lehigh (Class III, Pennsylvania): Located in a remote wilderness section of the state, the Lehigh offers over 30 miles of intermediate class whitewater. Early in the season the water coming out of the Pocono Mountains is very cold and wetsuits are a must.

Neversink (Class V+, New York): The Neversink, a tributary of the Delaware, has a 10-mile gorge between Bridgeville and Oakland Valley that is an exceptional challenge. Periodically, people try it, but few succeed.

Penobscot (Class IV, Maine): The West Branch of this river has 15 miles of fine wilderness floating. There is plenty of whitewater and wildlife to encounter, but there are active plans for a dam which will destroy this run if it is built.

Rappahannock (Class II, Virginia): The drift from Remington to Fredricksburg is a fine wilderness run, and only 50 miles from Washington, D. C. Your view from the river is forestland, with no farms or roads nearby for much of the float.

Withlacoochee (Class III, Georgia/Florida): This river is usually run in March, April and May for the best whitewater. The float from Highway 94 to the Suwannee River is 55 miles and in some places borders swamplands.

Loading the boats: The beginning of any multi-day float.

East Central Rivers

ALABAMA
Warrior-Locust Fork (Northern Alabama)

ARKANSAS
Buffalo (Northwestern Arkansas)
Cossatot (Southwestern Arkansas)

MINNESOTA
Kettle (Eastern Minnesota)

MISSOURI
St. Francis (Southeastern Missouri)

TENNESSEE
Ocoee (Southeastern Tennessee)
Hiwassee (Eastern Tennessee)

WEST VIRGINIA
Cheat (Northern West Virginia)
Gauley (Central West Virginia)
New-Lower Section (Central West Virginia)
New-Upper Section (Central West Virginia)

WISCONSIN
Flambeau (Northern Wisconsin)
Namekagon (Northwestern Wisconsin)
Peshtigo (Northeastern Wisconsin)
Wolf (Northeastern Wisconsin)
St. Croix (Wisconsin/Minnesota)

● Indicates extended description in text.

RIVER: *Buffalo*
LOCATION: Northwestern Arkansas
RUN: Ponca to Pruitt
DISTANCE: 25 miles
TIME: April to June
DIFFICULTY: Novice
RAPIDS: Wreckin' Rock (II), Gray Rock (II), Crisis Curve (II)
ENVIRONMENT: Forested hills and limestone bluffs
COMMENTS: This float is in the heart of the Ozark Mountains and is one of the finest canoe and scenery runs around. There are numerous places to explore ashore, most notably a 200-foot falls up a narrow, dead-end canyon called Hemmed-in-Hollow. At high water you can float above Ponca and the rapids are bigger. You can lengthen the Ponca to Pruitt float by taking out at Woolum Ford (50 miles total; the rapids are smaller below Pruitt).

RIVER: *Cheat*
LOCATION: Northern West Virginia
RUN: Albright to Jenkinsburg Bridge
DISTANCE: 11 miles
TIME: April to June
DIFFICULTY: Advanced
RAPIDS: Big Nasty (IV), Trap (IV), High Falls (IV)
ENVIRONMENT: Steep-walled mountain canyon
COMMENTS: This river is not controlled and is subject to radical changes in flow—above 3.5 feet it becomes very dangerous. The Cheat is a moderately difficult run, with almost continuous, intricate rapids (over three dozen Class III or better). The shuttle in part is slow-going and it's easy to miss turns. If you want a longer run take out at Lake Lynn State Park—you'll get 8 miles more river, but the last 5 are flatwater.

RIVER: *Cossatot*
LOCATION: Southwestern Arkansas
RUN: Forest Service Road No. 31 Bridge to Highway 4 Bridge
DISTANCE: 12 miles
TIME: March to June
DIFFICULTY: Advanced
RAPIDS: Four Steps (III), Esses (IV), Cossatot Falls (IV+)
ENVIRONMENT: Heavily logged forested mountain wilderness
COMMENTS: A relatively unknown river, if the water level is up it's one of the best in the area. There are numerous Class III riffles in this run, but the major rapid is Cossatot Falls which is a series of six drops (with eyes like Eye Opener, Washing Machine, and Whiplash).

Floating Whitewater Rivers

Deep in the Ouachita Mountains, the landscape is wild and magnificent, except for areas of logging activity.

RIVER: *Flambeau*
LOCATION: Northern Wisconsin
RUN: Nine-mile Creek to Flambeau Lodge
DISTANCE: 46 miles
TIME: May to September
DIFFICULTY: Novice
RAPIDS: Beaver Dam (II+), Cedar (II), Flambeau Falls (II)
ENVIRONMENT: Thick forestland
COMMENTS: Winding through Flambeau State Forest, the Flambeau River is a wonderful wilderness run—there is great scenery and lots of wildlife. There are over a dozen primitive campsites along this stretch, places to spend time enjoying the landscape. The Flambeau provides one of the finest canoe and fishing (muskie, northern pike, sturgeon, and so on) runs anywhere.

RIVER: *Gauley*
LOCATION: Central West Virginia
RUN: Summersville Dam to Omega Siding
DISTANCE: 25 miles
TIME: September to October
DIFFICULTY: Expert
RAPIDS: Pillow Rock (V), Lost Paddle (V), Sweet's Falls (V)
ENVIRONMENT: Deep forestland canyon
COMMENTS: One of the Eastern United States' finest runs, it's located deep in the Appalachian Mountains. When floated at higher water levels it's big water; at lower levels it is very technical. Because of extreme undercutting of large boulders and rock formations, the Gauley is always dangerous. The action is nearly continuous: There are over 100 rapids on this run, sixty at Class III or above. The last major rapid on this run has an intriguing name—"Pure Screaming Hell." For a shorter (13 mile) run you can take out at Peter's Creek, but be prepared for a hike.

RIVER: *Hiwassee*
LOCATION: Eastern Tennessee
RUN: Powerhouse Boat Ramp to Highway 411 Bridge
DISTANCE: 11 miles
TIME: May to October
DIFFICULTY: Novice/Intermediate
RAPIDS: Little Rock Island (II+), Funnel (II+), Devil's Shoals (II+)
ENVIRONMENT: Heavily crested rolling hills

COMMENTS: Designated a Tennessee State Wild and Scenic River, the rapids aren't big but the lush landscape is. If you want to shorten the trip you can take out one-half way at Reliance; the upper section has the interesting, more exciting whitewater. The water of the Hiwassee tends to be very cold—wetsuits are generally worn.

RIVER: *Kettle*
LOCATION: Eastern Minnesota
RUN: Banning State Park to Robinson Park
DISTANCE: 4 miles
TIME: May to September
DIFFICULTY: Novice/Intermediate
RAPIDS: Blueberry Slide (II+), Dragon's Tooth (II+), Hell's Gate (II+)
ENVIRONMENT: Forestland
COMMENTS: This river is characterized by dangerous undercuts in the gorge. The run is very short but the magnificent scenery more than compensates. The water level can change dramatically overnight—when it goes over 5 feet it becomes a Class IV, advanced level, river.

RIVER: *Namekagon*
LOCATION: Northwestern Wisconsin
RUN: Trego Dam to Riverside Landing
DISTANCE: 34 miles
TIME: April to September
DIFFICULTY: Practice
RAPIDS: Many minor rapids
ENVIRONMENT: Wilderness forestland
COMMENTS: This river is a tributary of the St. Croix and both rivers can be floated to extend your trip. The Namekagon is a narrow, fast river with forests lining both banks. It's an excellent float for admiring scenery or to practice whitewater skills. It's very popular with canoeists and fishermen.

RIVER: *New (Lower Section)*
LOCATION: Central West Virginia
RUN: Thurmond to Fayette Station Bridge
DISTANCE: 15 miles
TIME: May to October
DIFFICULTY: Advanced
RAPIDS: Lower Keeny (IV), Double Z (IV), Undercut Rock (IV)
ENVIRONMENT: Forested mountain foothills
COMMENTS: This section of the New provides plenty of scenery, like the upper section, and adds several difficult rapids. It is referred

to by many as the "Grand Canyon of the East." This lower section begins with 7½ miles of calm water, interrupted at 4½ miles by one rapid (aptly named "Surprise"). From the end of the calm, you will encounter a lot of great whitewater.

RIVER: *New (Upper Section)*
LOCATION: Central West Virginia
RUN: Prince to Thurmond
DISTANCE: 15 miles
TIME: May to October
DIFFICULTY: Novice
RAPIDS: Many minor rapids
ENVIRONMENT: Forested mountain foothills
COMMENTS: The upper section of the New has wonderful scenery without difficult rapids. It is a lively ride with some big waves and easily avoided holes. You can combine the upper and lower sections for a 30-mile float.

RIVER: *Ocoee*
LOCATION: Southeastern Tennessee
RUN: Dam to U. S. 64 Shoulder
DISTANCE: 6 miles
TIME: April to October
DIFFICULTY: Advanced
RAPIDS: Broken Nose (IV), Buzzsaw (III+), Powerhouse (IV)
ENVIRONMENT: Rural forested areas
COMMENTS: This run is very short, but very sweet, with nearly continuous rapids most of the way. Since a road follows alongside, you can conveniently run it twice in the same day. When the water level exceeds 4000 cfs, the Ocoee becomes an expert's Class V trip.

RIVER: *Peshtigo*
LOCATION: Northeastern Wisconsin
RUN: Forest Service 2131 Bridge to Marinette County Highway C Bridge
DISTANCE: 20 miles
TIME: April and May
DIFFICULTY: Advanced
RAPIDS: Ralton's Rip (III), Roaring (IV), Horse Race (IV)
ENVIRONMENT: Forestland
COMMENTS: This stretch on the Peshtigo has been described as the best whitewater run in Wisconsin, primarily because of Roaring Rapids (a challenging Class IV consisting of six separate drops). This river is floatable only during the high waters of spring, so you'll need to check water level carefully.

RIVER: *St. Croix*
LOCATION: Wisconsin/Minnesota
RUN: Riverside Landing to Nevers Dam Landing
DISTANCE: 74 miles
TIME: April to September
DIFFICULTY: Novice
RAPIDS: Big Reef (II), August Olson (II), Yellow Pine (II)
ENVIRONMENT: Sparsely populated forestland
COMMENTS: The St. Croix is a wide, clear river, with numerous minor rapids. It is very popular with canoeists and has been designated Wild and Scenic. There are many beautiful forest campsites. You can begin this float just below Trego Dam on the Namekagon, which adds another 34 miles (or at Wisconsin Highway 77 Bridge, which adds 18 miles).

RIVER: *St. Francis*
LOCATION: Southeastern Missouri
RUN: Highway 72 Bridge to Highway D Bridge
DISTANCE: 6 miles
TIME: April to July
DIFFICULTY: Intermediate
RAPIDS: Big Drop (III), Cat's Paw (III+), Double Drop (III)
ENVIRONMENT: Granite gorge through heavy forest
COMMENTS: Located in the Missouri Ozarks, the St. Francis offers a lot of whitewater in a fast six-mile run. Be aware that the St. Francis is subject to rapid, radical changes in water level. When the water level rises (and covers the lower water bridge at Highway D), this becomes a Class V float, for experts only. There are four other whitewater runs nearby, including one on Marble Creek, that range in difficulty from novice to expert.

RIVER: *Warrier, Locust Fork*
LOCATION: Northern Alabama
RUN: U. S. 79 Bridge to Nectar Covered Bridge
DISTANCE: 7 miles
TIME: April to June
DIFFICULTY: Intermediate
RAPIDS: Double Trouble (III+), Bullard Shoals (III), Powell Falls (III)
ENVIRONMENT: Rolling tree-covered hills
COMMENTS: An interesting Class III run, with lush tree-covered hills, covered bridges, and some nice holes. Be aware that boaters (and their vehicles) are not welcome on much of the privately-owned riverbank and there is a longstanding antagonism between river folks and the local citizenry.

RIVER: *Wolf*
LOCATION: Northeastern Wisconsin
RUN: Lily to Big Smoky Falls
DISTANCE: 38 miles
TIME: April to August
DIFFICULTY: Intermediate
RAPIDS: Ducknest (III), Upper Dalles (III), Dalles (III+)
ENVIRONMENT: Forestland
COMMENTS: One of the first rivers in the National Wild and Scenic Rivers System, the Wolf provides a rugged wilderness float. There are rapids interspersed with calm water over the entire 38 miles. Just below the put-in you will have to negotiate (usually through the center) a permanent log jam. There is a put-in on private property (Boy Scout Camp—ask for permission) if you want a shorter trip (16 miles).

Other East Central Rivers

Big Fork (Class I+, Minnesota): A beautiful run through tall timber, many people begin on the Bowstring River above Dora Lake. Much of the draw to this river is in its wildlife which includes bear, moose, and timber wolf.

Cacapon (Class III, West Virginia): A popular stretch for boating is the 21-mile, Capon Bridge to Largent section. This river originates as the Lost River which disappears underground for miles.

Cumberland, South Fork (Class IV, Tennessee/Kentucky): There are two sections of this river that are regularly run. The upper one (above Leatherwood Bridge) has many Class III (and one Class IV) rapids; below the bridge is novice water except for two falls which are usually portaged.

Current (Class II, Missouri): The Current winds through a sparsely populated part of the Ozarks and wildlife is abundant. Much of this river is regularly frequented by canoeists and fishermen.

Dry Fork (Class IV, West Virginia): The Dry Fork is a small river with only a brief spring rafting season. It provides an interesting 12-mile float with footbridges, old homesteads, and so on.

Obed (Class IV, Tennessee): This river is usually run from a put-in on Big Daddy Creek (2 miles to the Obed) to Nemo Bridge, a total of 13 miles. It runs through a magnificent deep gorge, pretty much inacessible on foot.

Ontonagon (Class II+, Michigan): The 60-mile run from Sparrow Rapids Campground to U. S. Highway 45 Bridge goes through the Ottawa National Forest. The last 8 miles of the run is almost continuous novice/intermediate class whitewater.

Potomac (Class II, West Virginia): This river has a very popular 3-mile run, from Dam Number Three to Sandy Hook, called the Needles. It offers nearly continuous whitewater.

Upper Iowa (Class I+, Iowa): The 54 mile run from Lime Springs to Decorah is a very popular place to float and fish. The current moves you along at a good pace, but there are no rapids of note.

West Central Rivers

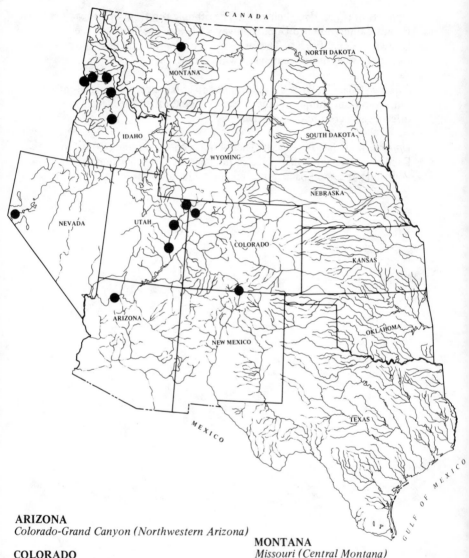

ARIZONA
Colorado-Grand Canyon (Northwestern Arizona)

COLORADO
Yampa (Northeastern Colorado)
Green-Upper Section (Colorado/Utah)
Rio Grande (Colorado/New Mexico)

IDAHO
Selway (Northern Idaho)
Salmon-Middle Fork (Central Idaho)
Salmon-Main (Central Idaho)
Salmon-Lower Gorge (Western Idaho)
Snake-Hells Canyon (Idaho/Oregon)

MONTANA
Missouri (Central Montana)

NEVADA
East Carson (Nevada/California)

UTAH
Green-Lower Section (Eastern Utah)
Green-Middle Section (Eastern Utah)

 Indicates extended description in text.

RIVER: *Colorado* (Grand Canyon)
LOCATION: Northwestern Arizona
RUN: Lee's Ferry to Diamond Creek
DISTANCE: 225 miles
TIME: April to October
DIFFICULTY: Expert
RAPIDS: Hance (V), Grapevine (V), Lava Falls (V+)
ENVIRONMENT: Immense desert canyon
COMMENTS: For most whitewater folks, the Colorado of the Grand Canyon is in a class all by itself. The river, the landscape, the experience are all exceptional. Permits are mandatory and there are many requirements (relating to boats, gear, and so on) that you will have to meet. There are over 100 rapids in this stretch, including Lava Falls, the nation's most famous whitewater. Everything is big on this river, especially the holes and the waves. Consequently, the craft that typically float the Colorado are also big, ranging to nearly 40 feet long.

RIVER: *East Carson*
LOCATION: Nevada/California
RUN: Hangman's Bridge to U. S. 395
DISTANCE: 20 miles
TIME: May and June
DIFFICULTY: Novice
RAPIDS: Many minor rapids
ENVIRONMENT: Mountain foothills to desert valley
COMMENTS: This river is mostly dependent upon spring runoff, so check water level. The take-out is a dirt road where the river comes close to U. S. 395, about 5 miles south of Gardnerville. Just below the take-out is a dangerous drop over a dam. When the water is high it is possible to begin this run at Wolf Creek and add 9 more miles and some class II+ action.

RIVER: *Green (Lower Section)*
LOCATION: Eastern Utah
RUN: Green River (town) to Colorado River
DISTANCE: 118 miles
TIME: All year
DIFFICULTY: Practice
RAPIDS: Many minor rapids
ENVIRONMENT: Desert canyonlands
COMMENTS: This is not a run for those seeking big whitewater. However, if you enjoy the desert wilderness, the landscape is magnificent. This stretch ends at the confluence of the Green with the

151

Floating Whitewater Rivers

Colorado River. If you continue downstream you'll enter Cataract
Canyon, which requires a permit and is for experts only. The end
part of this run is in the heart of Utah's Canyonlands.

RIVER: *Green* (Middle Section)
LOCATION: Eastern Utah
RUN: Sand Wash to Green River (town)
DISTANCE: 96 miles
TIME: All year
DIFFICULTY: Intermediate
RAPIDS: Coal Creek (III+), McPherson (III), Rattlesnake (III)
ENVIRONMENT: Sagebrush covered desert
COMMENTS: There are relatively few rapids on this run, with lots of
calm, flat-water floating. You'll go through Desolation Canyon and
Gray Canyon, both awesome desert wilderness gorges. This section
of the Green requires a permit. Although this river can be run all
year, the best time is in June and July.

RIVER: *Green* (Upper Section)
LOCATION: Colorado/Utah
RUN: Dutch John to Dinosaur National Monument Headquarters
DISTANCE: 90 miles
TIME: May to September
DIFFICULTY: Advanced
RAPIDS: Upper Disaster Falls (IV), Hell's Half Mile (IV), Moonshine
  (IV)
ENVIRONMENT: Sagebrush covered desert
COMMENTS: This section of the Green flows through the Dinosaur
National Monument and permits with strict boating guidelines are re-
quired. You begin your float in Utah, drift into Colorado, then finish
in Utah. The 90 miles takes you through Lodore, Whirlpool, and
Split Mountain Canyons, all arid and rocky. Each canyon has numer-
ous rapids to test a boatman's skill, over 60 in all. This trip can be
shortened by putting in or taking out the Gates of Lodore (just before Lodore Canyon) or Split Mountain Campground (just after
Split Mountain Canyon).

RIVER: *Missouri*
LOCATION: Central Montana
RUN: Fort Benton to Robinson Bridge
DISTANCE: 160 miles
TIME: April to October
DIFFICULTY: Novice
RAPIDS: Black Bluff (II), Deadman (II), Birch (II+)

ENVIRONMENT: Prairieland
COMMENTS: Truly a wilderness waterway, it belongs in the National Wild and Scenic Rivers System. Permits are required all summer. The broad, often lazy river winds through countless bluffs and buttes. There are numerous great campsites, usually nestled in willows and cottonwoods. The length of this trip can be shortened by putting in either at Loma Ferry or Virgelle Ferry.

RIVER: *Rio Grande*
LOCATION: Colorado/New Mexico
RUN: Lobatos Bridge to Lee Trail
DISTANCE: 24 miles
TIME: May to September
DIFFICULTY: Novice
RAPIDS: Many minor rapids
ENVIRONMENT: Semi-arid prairie flatlands
COMMENTS: The Rio Grande was one of the first rivers in the National Wild and Scenic Rivers System (in fact, it was the very first one formally dedicated as such). Permits are required for six specific sections. The Lobatos to Lee Trail stretch is one of many fine wilderness floats offered by this river. The various sections range from flatwater to Class V+—there is a run at any level you want. If you want a longer trip from Lobatos Bridge, you can float to Taos Junction (58 miles). As you leave Lee Trail, the canyon becomes deeper and the whitewater Class V to VI, for the most adventurous of experts only.

RIVER: *Salmon, Lower Gorge*
LOCATION: Western Idaho
RUN: Whitebird Bridge to confluence of Grande Ronde and Snake
DISTANCE: 70 miles
TIME: July to September
DIFFICULTY: Intermediate/Advanced
RAPIDS: Snohole (III+), China (III+), Bjerke's Boulder (III+)
ENVIRONMENT: Deep grass-covered desert canyon
COMMENTS: The lower Salmon provides big water rafting in a stark and vast wilderness. It usually is hot in the summer, over 100 degrees every day, and there are lots of beautiful white sand beaches for camping. The last 20 miles of this trip are on the Snake River and expect to run into lots of people, power boats, and so on.

RIVER: *Salmon, Main*
LOCATION: Central Idaho
RUN: Cache Bar to Vinegar Creek
DISTANCE: 86 miles

Floating Whitewater Rivers

TIME: June to September
DIFFICULTY: Intermediate/Advanced
RAPIDS: Ranier (III+), Big Mallard (III+), Elkhorn (III+)
ENVIRONMENT: Sloping, grassy hills; some forest and deep canyon
COMMENTS: The "River of No Return" runs through the second deepest canyon in the U.S. (over a thousand feet deeper than the Grand Canyon) and is the longest river located entirely in one state. The setting is awesome wilderness (it bisects the protected Idaho Primitive Area), with many magnificent campsites and plenty of wildlife. The shuttle is very long (nearly 400 miles)—either hire shuttle drivers or give yourself plenty of extra time. This section was designated Wild and Scenic in 1980—permits are required.

RIVER: *Salmon, Middle Fork*
LOCATION: Central Idaho
RUN: Dagger Falls to Cache Bar
DISTANCE: 99 miles
TIME: July and August
DIFFICULTY: Advanced
RAPIDS: Velvet (IV), Pistol Creek (III+), Rubber (IV)
ENVIRONMENT: Deep canyons and forested hills
COMMENTS: There are over 300 rapids in 99 magnificent wilderness miles. The river is designated Wild and Scenic and permits are required. It is surrounded by a one-million-plus acre Idaho Primitive Area, the largest undeveloped land mass in the contiguous 48 states. Wildlife, clean air, clear water and beautiful campsites abound. Be particularly alert to water level as it can change overnight. In June, 1970, several floaters found themselves on the river at very high water levels and six people died (on the Middle Fork and Main combined).

RIVER: *Selway*
LOCATION: Northern Idaho
RUN: Paradise to Selway Falls
DISTANCE: 49 miles
TIME: June and July
DIFFICULTY: Advanced/Expert
RAPIDS: Ladle (IV), Teekum Falls (IV), Wolf Creek (IV)
ENVIRONMENT: Pristine forested wilderness
COMMENTS: A fast-moving river with numerous rapids, including six Class IV's and ten Class III's. At the time of this writing only one launch is allowed per day, so you don't see many people on the river. Be particularly alert to changing water levels, especially in smaller boats. You'll get wet and the water temperature can be below 40 degrees, so plan accordingly.

RIVER: *Snake (Hell's Canyon)*
LOCATION: Idaho/Oregon
RUN: Hell's Canyon Dam to State Park
DISTANCE: 78 miles
TIME: June to September
DIFFICULTY: Advanced/Expert
RAPIDS: Wild Sheep Creek (IV+), Cache (IV+), Rush Creek (IV)
ENVIRONMENT: Semi-arid deep canyon
COMMENTS: Partly designated wild, the rest scenic, permits are required. On this portion of the Snake (the entire river is over 1000 miles long) you will float through the deepest canyon in North America. Except for the first 16 miles expect to encounter jet boats coming up from Lewiston. This river, especially after the Salmon joins it (after 58 miles of drifting), carries a tremendous volume of water. Most people run it at its very lowest, less than 15,000 cfs, at Hell's Canyon gauge—at other times it can exceed 35,000 cfs.

RIVER: *Yampa*
LOCATION: Northeastern Colorado
RUN: Deerlodge Park to Echo Park
DISTANCE: 47 miles
TIME: May to July
DIFFICULTY: Advanced
RAPIDS: Teepee (IV), Big Joe (III), Warm Springs (IV)
ENVIRONMENT: Semi-arid sandstone canyons
COMMENTS: This float is mostly within the Dinosaur National Monument and permits are required. The 47 miles ends at the confluence of the Yampa and the Green; from here you can continue on the Green (to the Split Mountain boat ramp) to lengthen your trip to 72 miles. This run is popular with boaters who like multi-day stretches of river.

Other West Central Rivers

Coeur d'Alene (Class II, Idaho): The upper section of this river is a popular stretch for canoes. The optimum water levels usually occur in late spring and early summer.

Deadwood (Class V, Idaho): This river offers a kayaks only, 25 mile stretch of very technical Class V water. It flows through a deep, narrow gorge in remote wilderness.

Flathead (Class IV, Montana): Whitewater enthusiasts run both the North and South Forks of this river (and occasionally the Middle

Floating Whitewater Rivers

Fork). The South has a tough portage below Black Bear Creek, the North has more large rapids.

Gila (Class IV, Arizona/New Mexico): There are several stretches of this river which can be run, but be especially concerned about river level. A wilderness permit is required on the uppermost section.

Greys (Class II+, Wyoming): This is a high-country river with numerous intermediate rapids in the stretch from Corral Creek Station to Lynx Creek Campground. Below Lynx Creek is Class V to unrunnable whitewater.

Little White (Class II, South Dakota): The Little White, from Ghost Hawk Campground to Highway 83, meanders through grassy rolling hills. There's a stretch in the middle of the run where fallen trees and scrub brush along the banks will slow you up.

Madison (Class III+, Montana): There are two stretches often run on this river. Above Ennis Dam is easy floating, but below the dam is some challenging whitewater.

North Platte (Class III, Wyoming/Colorado): The best time to run this river is in May, June or July. It is best floated in craft appropriate for high-volume technical whitewater.

Payette (Class V, Idaho): There are several stretches on the middle and south forks and the main river offering excellent whitewater. You can find a run at any level of difficulty you choose.

Priest (Class III, Idaho): High in the panhandle of Idaho, there is some great scenery and intermediate level whitewater. This river becomes very dangerous at high water.

Salt (Class IV, Arizona): The 52-mile stretch from Highway 60 to Highway 288 is a wilderness run with several tough sections of whitewater. Attempt this run from May to July to ensure sufficient water.

San Juan (Class III+, Utah): Permits are required for this beautiful desert run in southern Utah. The river becomes unrunnable after midsummer in dry years.

West Coast Rivers

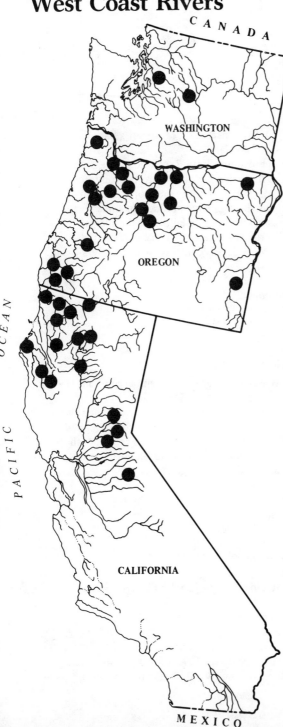

WASHINGTON
South Fork Skykomish (Northern Washington)
Wenatchee (Central Washington)

OREGON
Grande Ronde (Northeastern Oregon)
Nehalem (Northwestern Oregon)
Sandy (Northwestern Oregon)
Clackamas-Lower Section (N.W. Oregon)
Clackamas-Upper Section (N.W. Oregon)
John Day-Lower Section (North-Central Oregon)
John Day-Upper Section (Central Oregon)
Crooked (Central Oregon)
Deschutes-Lower Section (Central Oregon)
Deschutes-Upper Section (Central Oregon)
McKenzie (Western Oregon)
North Santiam (Western Oregon)
South Santiam (Western Oregon)
Illinois (Southwestern Oregon)
Owyhee-Lower Section (Southeastern Oregon)
Owyhee-Upper Section (Southeastern Oregon)
Rogue-Lower Section (Southwestern Oregon)
Rogue-Upper Section (Southwestern Oregon)
North Umpqua (Southwestern Oregon)

CALIFORNIA
Salmon (Northwestern California)
Trinity (Northwestern California)
Eel, Main-Lower Section (N.W. California)
Eel, Main-Upper Section (N.W. California)
Middle Fork Eel (Northwestern California)
North Fork Smith (Northwestern California)
Klamath-Lower Section (Northern California)
Klamath-Middle Section (Northern California)
Sacramento-Lower Section (N. California)
Sacramento-Upper Section (N. California)
McCloud (Northern California)
Scott (Northern California)
South Fork American (Northern California)
North Fork American (Central California)
Middle Fork American (Central California)
Tuolumne (Central California)

● Indicates extended description in text

Floating Whitewater Rivers

RIVER: *American, Middle Fork*
LOCATION: Central California
RUN: Oxbow Bend to North Fork
DISTANCE: 26 miles
TIME: May to September
DIFFICULTY: Expert
RAPIDS: Tunnel Chute (V), Cartwheel (IV), Murderer's Bar (V)
ENVIRONMENT: Mountain forestland
COMMENTS: Located in the Auburn State Recreation Area in the
Sierra Nevadas, you'll travel through a beautiful forested canyon.
The water is clear and generally very cool. At one point, Ruck-A-
Chucky Rapid, the river flows through large boulders in three steep
drops—portage will be necessary and can be laborious with larger
boats. The take-out for this run is at the confluence of the Middle
Fork and the North Fork. (Most details courtesy of Headwaters River
Adventures, Ashland, Oregon)

RIVER: *American, North Fork*
LOCATION: Central California
RUN: Robbers Ravine to Ponderosa Way
DISTANCE: 9 miles
TIME: April to June
DIFFICULTY: Advanced
RAPIDS: Staircase (IV), Bogus Thunder (IV), Chamberlain Falls (IV)
ENVIRONMENT: Mountain forestland
COMMENTS: This river is one of the few remaining undammed rivers
in the Sierra Nevada mountain range, in Mother Lode country. Fed by
snowmelt, plan for a cold water run. There are lots of rapids, with
several to test the experienced floater. (Most details courtesy of
Headwaters River Adventures, Ashland, Oregon)

RIVER: *American, South Fork*
LOCATION: Northern California
RUN: Chili Bar to Salmon Falls Bridge
DISTANCE: 20 miles
TIME: May to September
DIFFICULTY: Advanced
RAPIDS: Troublemaker Rapids (IV), Hospital Falls (III), Satan's
Cesspool (IV)
ENVIRONMENT: Steep rocky canyons, pine-covered hills
COMMENTS: This run has some great names for rapids (like those
above, and Meatgrinder, Old Scary, Triple Threat, and Recovery
Room) and one mistake will indicate why. As of this writing, permits
are required for commercial groups only; BLM asks for a voluntary

registration by private boaters. River level fluctuates quite a bit as water is released from Chili Bar Dam. Most of the land you float by, on both sides, is privately owned. For a shorter run you can take-out or put-in midway at Camp Lotus.

RIVER: *Clackamas, Lower Section*
LOCATION: Northwestern Oregon
RUN: McIver Park to Riverside Park
DISTANCE: 16 miles
TIME: May to July
DIFFICULTY: Novice
RAPIDS: Many minor rapids
ENVIRONMENT: Moderately populated, partially forested
COMMENTS: This run is very accessible to the Portland metro area and consequently can get very crowded. It is an excellent stretch of river for novices and for open canoes. Generally, the water is very cold—that coupled with cool, cloudy days increases the potential for hypothermia hazards.

RIVER: *Clackamas, Upper Section*
LOCATION: Northwestern Oregon
RUN: Indian Henry Camp turnoff to North Fork Reservoir
DISTANCE: 13 miles
TIME: May to July
DIFFICULTY: Advanced
RAPIDS: Powerhouse (III+), Toilet Bowl (III+), Carter Bridge Falls (IV)
ENVIRONMENT: Forested canyon
COMMENTS: This section is on the beautiful forested western slope of the Cascade mountain range. The river is primarily snowmelt and so wetsuits are highly recommended. Be aware that there are varying spots for both put-in and take-out and that some hauling up and down steep banks may be required.

RIVER: *Crooked*
LOCATION: Central Oregon
RUN: Lone Pine Bridge to Lake Billy Chinook Bridge
DISTANCE: 20 miles
TIME: April and May
DIFFICULTY: Expert
RAPIDS: Wap-te-doodle (V+), No Name (V), Chinese Dam (V+)
ENVIRONMENT: High desert
COMMENTS: The Crooked River is said by many to be in a league with Oregon's Illinois and Upper Owyhee rivers. It has numerous big

Floating Whitewater Rivers

rapids and winds through a spectacular gorge. It is for experts only. Crooked River Ranch offers camping facilities in the middle of this stretch—if you spend time scouting, it's always a two-day run. The floating season on this river is very short, and some years is non-existent.

RIVER: *Deschutes, Lower Section*
LOCATION: Central Oregon
RUN: Mack's Canyon to Columbia River
DISTANCE: 24 miles
TIME: April to December
DIFFICULTY: Intermediate/Advanced
RAPIDS: Gordon Ridge (III+), Rattlesnake (III+), Moody (III)
ENVIRONMENT: High desert hills
COMMENTS: This section of the Deschutes is only a little easier than the upper section, and similar in terrain. If you wish to extend the trip, you can put in a little below Sherars Falls (making the mileage 43). Campsites are often difficult to obtain during peak use times. The take-out is at Deschutes River Park; head left as you meet the Columbia.

RIVER: *Deschutes (Upper Section)*
LOCATION: Central Oregon
RUN: Highway 26 Bridge to Swimming Hole
DISTANCE: 54 miles
TIME: April to December
DIFFICULTY: Advanced
RAPIDS: Whitehorse (IV), Train Hole (IV), Oak Springs (IV)
ENVIRONMENT: High desert hills
COMMENTS: The Deschutes is one of the busiest rivers in the Northwest (some estimates of its summer use exceed 60,000 people). The terrain is high desert, with sagebrush and junipers, and much of the riverbank is privately owned (including the Warm Springs Indian Reservation on the left part of the way). Campsites are sometimes at a premium, so plan ahead. The take-out is Swimming Hole (on the right) a couple of miles before Sherars Falls (a dangerous Class VI).

RIVER: *Eel, Main (Lower Section)*
LOCATION: Northwestern California
RUN: Alderpoint to Fort Seward
DISTANCE: 8 miles
TIME: April to June
DIFFICULTY: Practice
RAPIDS: Many minor rapids

ENVIRONMENT: Partially forested with deep gorges
COMMENTS: This section is not for those seeking the thrills of big whitewater. However, if you want scenery, relaxation, or a place to practice your boating skills, it is a beautiful drift. It can be combined with the Upper Section of the Main Eel to make a 54-mile trip.

RIVER: *Eel, Main (Upper Section)*
LOCATION: Northwestern California
RUN: Dos Rios to Alderpoint
DISTANCE: 46 miles
TIME: April to June
DIFFICULTY: Intermediate
RAPIDS: Spyrock (III), Island Mountain Falls (III), Kekawaka Falls (III)
ENVIRONMENT: Partially forested with deep gorges
COMMENTS: Convenient to the San Francisco Bay area, the Eel flows out of coastal range mountains over 200 miles to the Pacific Ocean. The river is lined with craggy rock sculptures unique to that part of California. Wildlife is abundant, especially deer and many varieties of birds. Be alert to tremendous fluctuations in water level, especially during spring rains. (Most details courtesy of Headwaters River Adventures, Ashland, Oregon)

RIVER: *Eel, Middle Fork*
LOCATION: Northwestern California
RUN: Black Butte River to Dos Rios
DISTANCE: 30 miles
TIME: April to May
DIFFICULTY: Advanced/Expert
RAPIDS: Skinny Chute (IV), Coal Mine Falls (V), Swallow Rock (IV)
ENVIRONMENT: Coastal mountain forestland
COMMENTS: The Middle Fork of the Eel has recently been designated Wild and Scenic, and represents the longest stretch of roadless wilderness river in the state of California. The forests are tall and thick and wildlife abounds. Carefully scout Coal Mine Falls; at certain water levels you will have to portage. The put-in is at the confluence with Black Butte River and the take-out is at the confluence of the forks of the Eel. (Most details courtesy of Headwaters River Adventures, Ashland, Oregon)

RIVER: *Grande Ronde*
LOCATION: Northeastern Oregon
RUN: Minam State Park to Troy Bridge
DISTANCE: 44 miles

TIME: June and July (also January and February)
DIFFICULTY: Intermediate
RAPIDS: Blind Falls (II), Sheep Creek (III), Martin's Misery (III)
ENVIRONMENT: Heavily forested deep canyons
COMMENTS: The first eight miles of this run is on the Wallowa River. The Grande Ronde is a relatively untravelled river and campsites are numerous and very pleasant. In contrast to the drop and pool character of most northwestern whitewater rivers, the Grande Ronde has a fairly constant slope (slightly over 20 feet per mile).

RIVER: *Illinois*
LOCATION: Southwestern Oregon
RUN: Oak Flat to Rogue River
DISTANCE: 34 miles
TIME: March to May
DIFFICULTY: Expert
RAPIDS: Pine Creek (IV+), Green Wall (V), Submarine Hole (IV+)
ENVIRONMENT: Coastal mountain range
COMMENTS: A beautiful wilderness river, the Illinois is for experts. There are over 100 rapids Class II or better, with 11 Class IV, IV+, or V. This river is strewn with uncounted boulders, making it a difficult technical run. The landscape is lush coastal forests, and wildlife abounds. Be aware that the Illinois is subject to rapid fluctuations in level during its floating season.

RIVER: *John Day (Lower Section)*
LOCATION: Northcentral Oregon
RUN: Clarno Bridge to Cottonwood Bridge
DISTANCE: 70 miles
TIME: April to June
DIFFICULTY: Novice/intermediate.
RAPIDS: Clarno (III), Basalt (II+)
ENVIRONMENT: High desert
COMMENTS: Only because of Clarno Rapids is this section more difficult than the Upper Section. If you portage Clarno, it actually is a little easier. This section also has designation as a Scenic Waterway, quite a few primitive campsites, and tremendous water level fluctuation at times.

RIVER: *John Day (Upper Section)*
LOCATION: Central Oregon
RUN: Service Creek to Clarno Bridge
DISTANCE: 46 miles
TIME: April to June

DIFFICULTY: Novice
RAPIDS: Russo (II+), Wreck (II), Burnt Ranch (II)
ENVIRONMENT: High desert
COMMENTS: This river is not regulated by a dam and thus is subject to wide fluctuations in water level. It has designation as a Scenic Waterway. The campsites are ample but primitive. This is a popular, non-difficult run for intermediates and advanced novices, recommended for anyone who loves the desert.

RIVER: *Klamath (Lower Section)*
LOCATION: Northern California
RUN: Happy Camp to Green Riffle
DISTANCE: 36 miles
TIME: May to October
DIFFICULTY: Intermediate/advanced
RAPIDS: Rattlesnake (III+), Devil's Toenail (III+), Dragon Tooth (IV)
ENVIRONMENT: Semi-arid, partially forested hills
COMMENTS: An exciting float with plenty of sun, wildlife and rapids. You'll see many reminders of mining from the late 1800s and the side-trip up Ukonom Creek to the falls is more than worth the time. A road follows alongside this entire stretch. There are many more miles of boatable whitewater below Ishi Pishi Falls (unrunnable) including the three Ike's rapids just below the Klamath's confluence with the Salmon.

RIVER: *Klamath (Middle Section)*
LOCATION: Northern California
RUN: Klamathon to Beaver Creek Lodge
DISTANCE: 22 miles
TIME: May to October
DIFFICULTY: Intermediate
RAPIDS: Honolulu (III), Schoolhouse (III), Dutch Creek (III)
ENVIRONMENT: Semi-arid, partially forested hills
COMMENTS: There are many remains of mining from around the turn of the century, and various kinds of wildlife on this run. Camping areas are very limited but pleasant. During the summer months be prepared to share the river with numerous dredging operations. The take-out is at a private lodge; contact them ahead for permission. A road follows along and above the river for this entire section. For a shorter run you can put-in or take-out midway at Tree of Heaven Park.

RIVER: *McCloud*
LOCATION: Northern California

RUN: Lower Falls Campground to McCloud Reservoir
DISTANCE: 6 miles
TIME: May to July
DIFFICULTY: Novice/intermediate
RAPIDS: Upper Big Springs (II+), Crystal Hallway (II's and III's), Merlin's Wall (II+)
ENVIRONMENT: Mountain forestland
COMMENTS: This river is fed by the glaciers of Mt. Shasta and provides a wonderful day run, in part through massive virgin pine forests. Wetsuits should be worn as the water is extremely cold. Over 90 percent of this run is through private property, so be very careful to float with no environmental impact.

RIVER: *McKenzie*
LOCATION: Western Oregon
RUN: Blue River to Leaburg Dam
DISTANCE: 18 miles
TIME: May to November
DIFFICULTY: Novice/intermediate
RAPIDS: Deer Creek (II), Martin Creek (III), Gate Creek (II+)
ENVIRONMENT: Sparsely populated forested hills
COMMENTS: The McKenzie has long been a favorite for drift boat fishermen, and it's located close to the Eugene metro area. It's a relatively easy run, with the exception of Martin Creek Rapids—this one can be dangerous if you aren't paying attention.

RIVER: *Nehalem*
LOCATION: Northwestern Oregon
RUN: Spruce Run Park to Nehalem Falls
DISTANCE: 16 miles
TIME: April to June
DIFFICULTY: Intermediate
RAPIDS: Little Falls (III), Salmonberry Drop (III), Nehalem Falls (III+)
ENVIRONMENT: Lush coastal forestland
COMMENTS: This run is convenient to the Portland metro area, yet is not overcrowded. The Nehalem cuts through high, heavily forested hills, rugged and only sparsely populated. Be certain to scout Nehalem Falls near the end of the run—it becomes unrunnable at very low water levels.

RIVER: *North Santiam*
LOCATION: Western Oregon
RUN: Packsaddle Park to Mehama Bridge

DISTANCE: 16 miles
TIME: February to November
DIFFICULTY: Intermediate
RAPIDS: Whitewater Challenge (II), Spencer's Hole (III), Mill City
   Bridge (III)
ENVIRONMENT: Sparsely populated forested hills
COMMENTS: Check the water level in late summer as it sometimes
drops too low. Also, check the water temperature—sometimes it is
very cold and wetsuits should be worn. It is possible to continue
downriver from Mehama Bridge, but you'll have to portage a fish
ladder.

RIVER: *Owyhee (Lower Section)*
LOCATION: Southeastern Oregon
RUN: Rome to Leslie Gulch
DISTANCE: 62 miles
TIME: April to June
DIFFICULTY: Intermediate/advanced
RAPIDS: Whistling Bird (III+), Montgomery (III), Rock Dam (III+)
ENVIRONMENT: Deep desert canyon
COMMENTS: A magnificent run for those who appreciate the desert.
The landscape varies in appearance from sagebrush-covered hills to
carved multicolor rock formations to near vertical narrow black rock
canyons. There are numerous small rapids (over 30 II's and II+'s),
plenty of campsites, and some interesting stops and side trips. The
last 10 miles is the Owyhee Reservoir and can be tough rowing if you
meet a headwind.

RIVER: *Owyhee (Upper Section)*
LOCATION: Southeastern Oregon
RUN: Three Forks to Rome
DISTANCE: 35 miles
TIME: May and June
DIFFICULTY: Expert
RAPIDS: Ledge (V), Halfmile (V), Widowmaker (VI)
ENVIRONMENT: High desert canyon
COMMENTS: This section of the Owyhee provides a tough run even
for experts. Widowmaker Rapid is aptly named and requires a back-
breaking and difficult portage if you want to avoid it. The desert
wilderness is beautiful and you'll likely encounter desert wildlife. Be
alert to highly variable weather and temperatures during the short
boating season.

RIVER: *Rogue (Lower Section)*
LOCATION: Southwestern Oregon

RUN: Grave Creek to Foster Bar
DISTANCE: 34 miles
TIME: May to October
DIFFICULTY: Advanced
RAPIDS: Rainie Falls (VI), Mule Creek Canyon (IV), Blossom Bar (IV)
ENVIRONMENT: Forested coastal mountain range
COMMENTS: Designated Wild and Scenic, permits are required for the lower section from June to September. Controlled by a dam, it often is runnable outside of permit season, but subject to moderate flooding after heavy rain. There are ample campsites, waterfalls, wildlife, and interesting side-trips including Zane Grey's cabin and a natural water slide at Tate Creek. There are a few lodges strategically placed along this otherwise wilderness river for floaters who would like to avoid meal preparation and camping.

RIVER: *Rogue (Upper Section)*
LOCATION: Southwestern Oregon
RUN: Hog Creek to Grave Creek
DISTANCE: 12 miles
TIME: All year
DIFFICULTY: Novice
RAPIDS: Dunn Riffle (II), Upper Galice (II+), Lower Galice (II)
ENVIRONMENT: Partially wooded low population area
COMMENTS: A beautiful day trip on a section of the Rogue River designated Scenic. There is heavy use during the summer months, averaging several hundred floaters per day. The scenery is good, featuring narrow rock canyons and thick forests. This section is excellent for steelhead, salmon and trout fishing.

RIVER: *Sacramento (Lower Section)*
LOCATION: Northern California
RUN: Redding to Red Bluff
DISTANCE: 55 miles
TIME: June to October
DIFFICULTY: Practice
RAPIDS: Many minor rapids
ENVIRONMENT: Big valley farmland
COMMENTS: This is not a wilderness run, nor one of heavy whitewater adventure. The river is big and wide on this stretch, averaging nearly 20,000 cfs during the summer and early fall months. It meanders through central California farmland but your view from the river is reasonably uncluttered by signs of people. The Sacramento is a great river for novices to practice rowing or paddling.

RIVER: *Sacramento (Upper Section)*
LOCATION: Northern California
RUN: Castle Crags to Dog Creek
DISTANCE: 23 miles
TIME: April to June
DIFFICULTY: Intermediate/advanced
RAPIDS: Staircase (III+), Whitehorse (III+), Shotgun (III+)
ENVIRONMENT: Pine-forested hills
COMMENTS: This run is on the upper reaches of the Sacramento River. There are numerous rapids to float in these 23 miles where the river is narrow and fast. Interstate 5 is nearby and is sometimes visible; otherwise, it's a sparkling clear river in a beautiful canyon with Mt. Shasta towering nearby. (Most details courtesy of Headwaters River Adventures, Ashland, Oregon)

RIVER: *Salmon (California)*
LOCATION: Northwestern California
RUN: Methodist Creek to Orleans
DISTANCE: 34 miles
TIME: April to July
DIFFICULTY: Expert
RAPIDS: Cascade (V), Butler's Lodge (V), Freight Train (V)
ENVIRONMENT: Coastal forestland
COMMENTS: There are more than five dozen rapids on this run, several of them Class V's—this stretch for experts only. The majority of the 34 miles is on the Salmon, with the last few miles on the Klamath. To shorten the run you can put in at Butler Flat (16 miles, and the Class V's are avoided), or Forks of the Salmon (26 miles). The Salmon's tougher sections are boulder-choked narrow canyons. (Most details courtesy of Headwaters River Adventures, Ashland, Oregon)

RIVER: *Sandy*
LOCATION: Northwestern Oregon
RUN: Dodge Park to Dabney Park
DISTANCE: 12 miles
TIME: April to June
DIFFICULTY: Intermediate
RAPIDS: Pipeline (IV), Mine Field (III), Whoopdeedo (III)
ENVIRONMENT: Rocky forested canyon
COMMENTS: A great day trip for people in the metropolitan Portland area. The water is generally very cold and wetsuits are recommended. For the most part, the Sandy is a technical run, requiring a lot of maneuvering around rocks and holes. Located close to a heavily populated area, there is a remarkable amount of wildlife.

Floating Whitewater Rivers

RIVER: *Scott*
LOCATION: Northern California
RUN: Canyon Creek to Hamburg
DISTANCE: 18 miles
TIME: April to June
DIFFICULTY: Advanced/expert
RAPIDS: Thompson Creek (IV+), Whitehouse (IV+), Schuler's
Gulch (IV+)
ENVIRONMENT: Lush coastal forest
COMMENTS: The Scott is a fast and furious tributary feeding into
the Klamath River, and the last couple of miles on this run are actually
on the Klamath. The Scott offers a number of top-notch Class IV+
rapids. This area in northwestern California is magnificent, and the
river runs through smooth-walled rock canyon lined with lush groves
of conifers and oaks, with small grassy meadows perfect for campsites. Be particularly alert to water level changes which can radically
affect the difficulty of the run. (Most details courtesy of Headwaters
River Adventures, Ashland, Oregon)

RIVER: *Skykomish, South Fork*
LOCATION: Northern Washington
RUN: Sunset Falls to Highway 2 Bridge
DISTANCE: 8 miles
TIME: May to July, September and October
DIFFICULTY: Advanced
RAPIDS: Anderson (III+), Boulder Drop (IV+), Lunch Hole (III+)
ENVIRONMENT: Mountain forestland
COMMENTS: This river flows off the west side of the Cascade
Mountain Range. The water is generally very cold, and often so is
the air temperature—wetsuits are a must. Also, expect precipitation
and if you're lucky you'll be wrong. The landscape, including two
nearby mountain peaks, is absolutely beautiful. There are over a
dozen Class III or better rapids in this short day-run.

RIVER: *Smith, North Fork*
LOCATION: Northwestern California
RUN: Moore's Crossing to South Fork
DISTANCE: 21 miles
TIME: April to June
DIFFICULTY: Advanced
RAPIDS: Several unnamed Class III+s and IV's
ENVIRONMENT: Coastal forestland
COMMENTS: The North Fork of the Smith has a relatively short
season, depending on spring rains, and doesn't draw big crowds.

After the forks merge and it nears the ocean, the river widens and during certain times of the year you'll encounter a lot of fishermen, both in boats and on the bank. The water is generally very clear and a beautiful bright blue-green color. This run has dozens of complex, boulder-strewn rapids that make for an exciting technical run. (Most details courtesy of Headwaters River Adventures, Ashland, Oregon)

RIVER: *South Santiam*
LOCATION: Western Oregon
RUN: Foster Dam to Waterloo Bridge
DISTANCE: 14 miles
TIME: March to May
DIFFICULTY: Novice
RAPIDS: Many minor rapids
ENVIRONMENT: Sparsely populated forested hills
COMMENTS: An excellent run for novices in the Willamette Valley of Oregon, with over two dozen minor rapids. Take out before Waterloo Falls. Be alert to cold water on cold days—wetsuits should be worn.

RIVER: *Trinity*
LOCATION: Northwestern California
RUN: North Fork to Cedar Flat
DISTANCE: 23 miles
TIME: May to September
DIFFICULTY: Intermediate/advanced
RAPIDS: Hell Hole (III+), Fishtail (III+), The Slot (III+)
ENVIRONMENT: Pristine forestland
COMMENTS: The Trinity flows through what is regularly billed as one of the most beautiful canyons in California. This 23-mile stretch has a lot of rapids of moderate difficulty to augment the great scenery. The take-out is just below Cedar Flat Bridge. If you continue on downstream, you'll enter Burnt Ranch Gorge. The next 8 miles is one of the toughest runs found anywhere, with numerous Class V+, boat-eating rapids. (Most details courtesy of Headwaters River Adventures, Ashland, Oregon)

RIVER: *Tuolumne*
LOCATION: Central California
RUN: Lumsden Campground to Ward's Ferry Bridge
DISTANCE: 18 miles
TIME: May to September
DIFFICULTY: Advanced/expert

RAPIDS: Harvest Hole (IV), Clavey Falls (V), Hell's Kitchen (IV)
ENVIRONMENT: Partially forested western slope of Sierra Nevada
COMMENTS: The Tuolumne is subject to a wide variation in flow and becomes very dangerous over 4000 cfs. At runnable levels it is one long boulder maze after another, with numerous major rapids. Fast becoming one of the most popular rivers in the West, it offers a beautiful wilderness trip. It has been recently designated Wild and Scenic and permits are required.

RIVER: *Umpqua, North Fork*
LOCATION: Southwestern Oregon
RUN: Boulder Flat to Cable Crossing
DISTANCE: 32 miles
TIME: April to August
DIFFICULTY: Intermediate/advanced
RAPIDS: Pinball (IV), Little Niagara (III), Island (III)
ENVIRONMENT: Heavily forested mountain canyon
COMMENTS: The North Umpqua is fed by a series of alpine lakes in the mountain range west of Roseburg, Oregon. As you float down the western slope of the Cascades, the landscape is lush and beautiful. The whitewater is challenging and virtually nonstop for the entire trip. (Most details courtesy of Headwaters River Adventures, Ashland, Oregon)

RIVER: *Wenatchee*
LOCATION: Central Washington
RUN: Icicle Creek Road Bridge to Wenatchee River Park
DISTANCE: 21 miles
TIME: May to August
DIFFICULTY: Intermediate
RAPIDS: Rock Garden (III), Gorilla Falls (III), Drunkard's Drop (III)
ENVIRONMENT: Mountain forestland
COMMENTS: This river is glacier fed, flowing east out of the north Cascade Mountains. The water is cold and wetsuits are recommended. You'll need to cover the 21 miles in a day as campsites are not available. This river is also run above Leavenworth where it is Class II, novice water.

Other West Coast Rivers

Kern (Class V, California): There are several stretches to run both above Lake Isabella and below it, varying in Class from III to V, about 45 miles in all. The upper section in some years is not runnable due to low water, and permits are required on both sections.

Kings (Class III+, California): The Kings is the largest wild river in the Sierras with a very popular 10-mile whitewater stretch from Garnet Dike Campground to Kirch Flat. There is a run above the campground that occasionally is attempted (Class V to unrunnable).

Humptulips (Class II, Washington): The whitewater on this river is secondary to the scenery. You will float through the lush, fern-covered Olympic rain forest for 20 miles.

Mokelumne (Class V, California): There are several sections of this river that can be run, ranging from Class II to Class V. The landscape is magnificent, with tall pine forests along much of this very scenic river.

Molalla (Class III, Oregon): The Molalla offers a 22-mile float with lots of intermediate class water from 8 miles above Glen Avon to the Highway 213 Bridge. This run gets steadily easier as you go downstream.

Pit (Class IV+, California): There are a number of fine whitewater runs on the Pit River, most of them pretty tough. The river is located between Mt. Lassen and Mt. Shasta and the countryside is strewn with volcanic rock.

Sauk (Class IV+, Washington): Near Seattle, this river offers two popular runs. The one from Bedal to Whitechuck (8 miles) is for intermediates; from Whitechuck to Clear Creek (7 miles) is for experts.

Skagit (Class III, Washington): The 10-mile Nehalem Powerhouse to Bacon Creek Campground stretch is wild both in scenery and rapids. It's in the Cascade Mountain Range, an area of tall timber and thick underbrush.

Snoqualmie (Class III+, Washington): This middle fork of this river is very popular with kayakers and expert canoeists. It is runnable generally only in May and June.

Tolt (Class III, Washington): Only 20 miles from Seattle, the Tolt offers a 6-mile-long intermediate run. There are numerous rapids from the put-in to the take-out on the Snoqualmie River.

Truckee (Class III, California/Nevada): This river, flowing out of Lake Tahoe, offers numerous Class II and Class II+ runs in the spring and summer. It's a narrow, low volume river, best suited for small boats.

171

Glossary

Back Ferry: Move laterally across the river by angling the boat and rowing or paddling backward (the bow is usually pointed more or less downstream to slow up the craft while moving sideways).

Bilge Pump: Pumping device powered by hand or electricity, used to remove water from inside boats.

Body Surfing: General term used to denote floating through rapids without benefit of a boat.

Bow Draw: Paddler's draw stroke made to the bow (rather than the middle of the boat), for turning with little effect on forward motion.

Brace: Paddling stroke where the paddler moves the face of the blade from the surface of the water downward, to prevent capsizing.

Broaching: Situation where a boat is washed up against a rock or steep bank and held there by the current (without wrapping).

Chute: General term used to describe a relatively narrow, fast water channel.

Class: Label given to indicate the difficulty and danger of a rapid, ranging from I (easy) to VI (unrunnable).

Closed-face Reel: Zebco-type fishing reel, characterized by a plate covering the spool of line.

Curler: Also called a reversal, a wave that curls back upstream (following a hole).

Cushion: Mass of water which piles up on the upstream side of an above the surface rock.

Denier: Weight measurement for fabric reflecting the coarseness of the thread used (in grams per 9000 meters of length).

Draw: Paddling stroke where the paddler reaches out sideways, blade face parallel to the boat, then pulls straight toward the side of the craft.

Drift Fishing: Common fishing technique where bait or lure is cast into current and allowed to move downstream.

D-ring: Metal "D" shaped rings, affixed with a nylon strap by stitching to small pieces of coated fabric, for glueing onto inflatables (for tie-on points).

Drop: Term used to denote an abrupt and definable decrease in water elevation, including waterfalls.

Dry Box: This term is used for a variety of rigid waterproof containers, most often large, aluminum ones.

Dry Suit: Entirely waterproof clothing with rubberized seals around the neck, wrists, and ankles.

Duffek: Refined paddler's stroke for turning into eddies.

Eddy: Section of water, most often along the bank or immediately downstream of boulders, that is moving in the opposite direction of the main current.

Eddy Line: Transition area or line between downstream flowing water and an eddy (upstream flowing water).

Entrapment: Situation where a boat or person is pinned by the river current in an immediately life-threatening predicament.

Ferry: Move laterally across the river (toward one bank or the other) by rowing or paddling with the boat angled (rather than pointed directly downstream or directly upstream).

Firepan: Metal container with sides 5 inches or more in height, used to contain camp and/or cooking fires.

Flip Lines: Short lengths of rope tied to one side of a raft to flip it back upright after capsizing.

Floatation Bag: Used with kayaks and canoes and made of vinyl, nylon, or inflatable boat material, it provides floatation for small craft.

Fly Reel: Simplest of all fishing reels, line is fed directly onto a large spool.

Forward Ferry: Move laterally across the river by angling the boat and forward rowing or paddling (the bow is usually pointed more or less upstream to slow up the craft while moving sideways).

Haystack: Also called a standing wave, a wave created by the river dropping over a ledge or rock (including one well below the surface of the river).

Hole: Depression immediately downstream of the flow of water over a near the surface rock.

Hydroplane: Fishing device which is designed to use the river current to hold a lure in a steady position in midstream.

Hypalon: Registered product of the DuPont Company, high quality, rubber-like coating for fabrics used in constructing inflatables.

Hypothermia: Human body's reaction to cold which can result in death if not treated.

Level Wind Reel: Fishing reel with the spool of line perpendicular to the rod, used extensively for trolling techniques.

Lining: Sending your boat through a rapid unmanned, controlling it with ropes from the shore.

Low Impact: Term used to describe river running, including camping, which has little or no adverse effect on the natural environment.

Neoprene: Medium quality synthetic rubber used for coating fabrics for inflatables.

Oarlock: Metal device set into oarstands, usually "U" shaped for whitewater applications, which holds the oar shaft for rowing.

Oar Stands: Also called oarlock stands, they are affixed to the raft frame to hold oarlocks or pins.

Oar Stop: Made from rubber or nylon, they encircle the oar shaft to keep oars from sliding through the oarlocks when the boatman releases his grip.
Obstacle: General term used to denote anything in the river that floaters should avoid.

PFD: Personal floatation device, any of a number of safety devices designed to keep the wearer from sinking below the surface of the water.
Pillow: Slight rise of water over a rock near the surface.
Pins and Clips: System for affixing oars by putting clips on the oarshafts which snap over pins (tholepins) placed in the oarstands.
Plunking: Still fishing where a large weight is used to keep bait from moving downstream with the current.
Pontoon: Most commonly a narrow, elongated inflatable tube (used for catarafts).
Portaging: Carrying your boat on shore around a section of whitewater.
Pry: The opposite of the more common draw stroke, a paddler puts the face of the blade against the side of the boat and moves it directly away from the craft.
Pulling: Term used to indicate rowing backward (reaching forward with the oar handles, then bringing them toward the body).
Pushing: Term used to indicate rowing forward (the oar handles, starting near the body, are moved toward the bow).
PVC: Polyvinyl chloride, a plastic-like material used in making inflatables.

Rapid: Definable stretch of whitewater, usually between two sections of calmer water.
Reversal: Also called a curler, a wave that curls back upstream (following a hole).
Riffle: Defined differently in various locales, but generally means a section of whitewater that is fairly shallow, bubbly water.
Rocker: Term used to denote the curvature of the bottom of the boat from bow to stern (generally, the flatter the more stable, and the more curved, the more maneuverable).
Roll: Variation of a sweeping brace stroke used by hard-shell kayakers to upright an upsidedown boat.
Rooster Tail: Vertical or near-vertical spray of water off the front of a rock.
Rubbing Strake: Also called chafe pads or chafe strips, added overlapping material for extra protection from chafing on inflatables.

Self-bailing Floor: Laced-in, inflatable floor which allows water in the boat to leak back into the river.
Shipping Oars: Bringing the oar blades alongside or into the boat to avoid hazards immediately next to the craft.

Shuttle: General term used to describe the moving of one or more vehicles to the take-out of a run so they will be there at the end of a float.

Spinning Reel: Common fishing reel on most rivers, it has an open face (line is controlled by a bail) and is designed for casting.

Spray Skirt: Flexible 360-degree apron that fits around a kayaker's waist and attaches to the lip of the cockpit of the boat, to prevent water from entering the kayak.

Standing Wave: Also called a haystack, a wave created by the river dropping over a ledge or rock (including one well below the surface of the river).

Strainer: Hazard in the river which allows water to pass through, but not a person or a boat.

Suck Hole: Large hole (followed by a sizeable reversal) that tends to keep a swimmer or boat circling around in it.

Sweep: Paddling stroke where the paddler moves the blade in a wide half-circle (rather than keeping it close to the boat).

Sweeping Brace: Paddler's brace stroke done in a wide half-circle, for up-righting a tipping boat.

Tailout: Series of waves at the base of a rapid.

Tailwave: Wave in the tailout at the base of a rapid.

Technical Rapid: Whitewater characterized by the need for one or more changes in lateral position due to hazards in midstream.

Throw Rope: General name for any coiled or bagged length of rope designed to be tossed to someone in danger.

Thwart: Inflatable cross tube which adds floatation and provides stiffness and consistent shape to rafts.

Tongue: Passageway between two obstacles, a "V" of smooth water with the base or point downstream.

Trolling: In river fishing, a technique characterized by letting line out downstream from the boat.

Waterproof Bag: Also called a river bag, any of a number of entirely watertight containers, usually made from the same material as inflatables.

Wave: Rise or definable upsurge of water, often the result of a drop a short ways upstream.

Wet Suit: Clothing made from synthetic rubber which offers protection from cold by holding and warming a thin layer of water between the wearer and the suit.

Whitewater: Aerated, disturbed water flow created when a river crashes into, around or over obstructions (including slower moving water).

Wrap: Situation occurring when a boat hits an above the surface rock, the upstream tube is forced underwater, the downstream side goes up and the river plays against the floor.

Bibliography

American Whitewater Affiliation. *American Whitewater* (periodical). Box 273, Powell Butte, Oregon 97753. (magazine for whitewater enthusiasts)

Angier, Bradford & Taylor, Zack. *Introduction to Canoeing.* Harrisburg, Pennsylvania: Stackpole Books, 1973. (basic guide for canoeists)

Arighi, Scott & Arighi, Margaret S. *Wildwater Touring.* New York: MacMillan Publishing, 1974. (general book for whitewater river runners with a focus on the Pacific Northwest)

Arman, Florence. *The Rogue: A River to Run.* Grants Pass, Oregon: Wildwood Press, 1982. (story of Glen Wooldridge, a commercial whitewater fishing guide for over 60 years)

Armstead, Lloyd D. *Whitewater Rafting Guide.* Herndon, Virginia: Candid Photo Corporation, 1979. (rivers and outfitters in the eastern United States)

Burrell, Bob & Davidson, Paul. *Wild Water: West Virginia.* Parsons, West Virginia: McClain Printing, 1972. (guidebook for several eastern rivers)

Canoe America Associates. *Canoe* (periodical). Box 597, Camden, Maine 04843. (magazine for canoeists and kayakers)

Carter, Randy. *Canoeing Whitewater.* Oakton, Virginia: Appalachian Books, 1974. (focussed on rivers in the Southeast)

Collins, Robert O. & Nash, Roderick. *The Big Drops.* San Francisco: Sierra Club Books, 1978. (fascinating descriptions of ten big rapids)

Davidson, James & Rugge, John. *The Complete Wilderness Paddler.* New York: Knopf, 1976. (information for canoeing and kayaking)

Evans, Jay & Anderson, Robert. *Kayaking.* Brattleboro, Vermont: Stephen Greene Press, 1975. (source of information specifically for kayakers)

Frank Amato Publications. *Salmon Trout Steelheader* (periodical). Box 02112, Portland, Oregon 97202. (magazine for fishermen which includes fishing rivers by boat)

Furrer, Werner. *Water Trails of Washington.* Edmonds, Washington: Signpost Books, 1971. (brief description for numerous runs in the state of Washington)

Garren, John. *Oregon River Tours.* Beaverton, Oregon: Touchstone Press, 1979. (detailed guidebook for a dozen Oregon rivers)

Huser, Verne. *River Running.* Chicago: Henry Regnery Company, 1975. (basic book for whitewater enthusiasts)

Jacobson, Cliff. *Canoeing Wild Rivers.* Merrillville, Indiana: ICS Books, Inc., 1984. (extensive sourcebook for canoeists)

Jenkinson, Michael. *Wild Rivers of North America.* New York: G. P. Dutton, 1981. (description of over 100 rivers in North America)

Kuhne, Cecil. *River Rafting.* Mountain View, California: World Publications, 1979. (basic book for rafting, including paddle rafting)

Malo, John. *Malo's Complete Guide to Canoeing and Canoe-camping.*

Chicago: Quadrangle Books, 1969. (resource book for canoeists)

Martin, Charles. *Sierra Whitewater.* Wayland, Massachusetts: Charles Fontaine Martin, 1974. (guidebook for northern and central California rivers)

Mays, Buddy. *Wildwaters.* San Francisco: Chronicle Books, 1977. (entertaining group of stories describing several river runs)

McGinnis, William. *Whitewater Rafting.* New York: Qudrangle, 1975. (book full of details for rafters and useful for all whitewater enthusiasts)

McNair, Robert E. *Basic River Canoeing.* Martinsville, Indiana: American Camping Association, 1972. (fundamentals for river running canoeists)

Miskimins, R. W. *Fishing Tips: Rogue River Steelhead.* Grants Pass, Oregon: GPSG, 1984. (techniques for steelhead fishing)

Miskimins, R. W. *Rogue River Guidebook: Hog Creek to Grave Creek.* Grants Pass, Oregon: GPSG, 1985. (guidebook for the popular middle Rogue River)

Nealy, William. *Whitewater Home Companion* (Southeastern Rivers). Hillsborough, North Carolina: Menasha Ridge Press, 1981. (entertaining and detailed guidebook for Southeastern rivers)

Ovington, Ray & Ovington, Moraima. *Canoeing Basics for Beginners.* Harrisburg, Pennsylvania: Stackpole Books, 1984. (canoeing fundamentals with emphasis on paddling techniques)

Rancher Publications. *River Runner* (periodical). Box 2047, Vista, California 92083. (magazine for whitewater enthusiasts)

Riviere, Bill. *Pole, Paddle and Portage: A Complete Guide to Canoeing.* New York: Van Nostrand Reinhold, 1973. (details for canoeists with rivers to run)

Sanders, William. *Kayak Touring.* Harrisburg, Pennsylvania: Stackpole Books, 1984. (floating kayaks both in rivers and in open water)

Sierra Club. *Sierra* (periodical). 530 Bush Street, San Francisco, California 94108. (emphasis on political and social action, it features occasional articles on rivers)

Steidle, Robert. *Wild-water Canoeing and Kayaking.* Paramus, New Jersey: Jolex, 1976. (a book for whitewater canoeists and kayakers)

Urban, John T. *A White-water Handbook for Canoe and Kayak.* Boston: Appalachian Mountain Club, 1973. (details of river running for paddlers)

Watters, Ron. *The White-water River Book.* Seattle: Pacific Search Press, 1982. (covers many and varied aspects of river running)

Whitney, P. D. *White-Water Sport: Running Rapids in Kayak and Canoe.* New York: Ronald Press, 1960. (focussed on whitewater river running for paddlers)

Ziff-Davis Publishing. *Backpacker* (periodical). One Park Avenue, New York, New York 10016. (primarily for backpackers, it features occasional articles on wilderness floating)

INDEX

A VIDEO TEXTBOOK

Fundamentals of Whitewater Rafting

by R. W. Miskimins

In the classroom and on the river, reading the river and rowing techniques are presented and discussed.

Future releases:

Fishing Techniques for Whitewater Boaters
Guide to Paddling Inflatable Kayaks
Environmental Images
575 South Espey Road
Grants Pass, Oregon 97527

More Useful Information

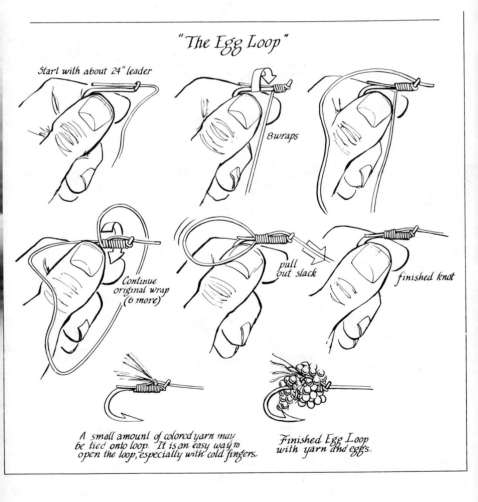

"The Egg Loop"

Start with about 24" leader

8 wraps

Continue original wrap (6 more)

pull out slack

finished knot

A small amount of colored yarn may be tied onto loop. It is an easy way to open the loop, especially with cold fingers.

Finished Egg Loop with yarn and eggs.

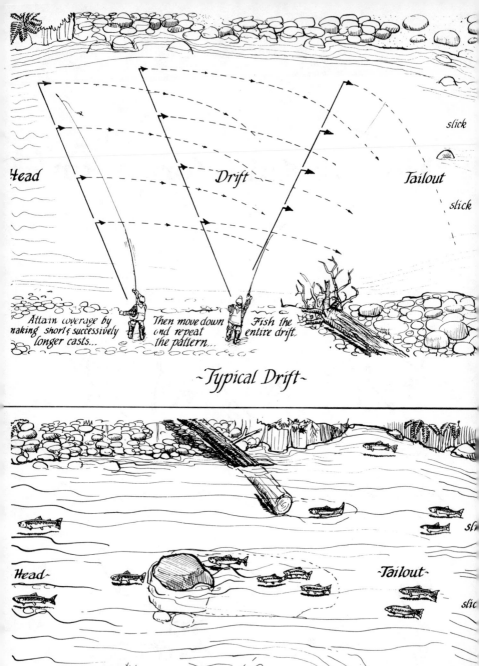

slick

Head   Drift   Tailout

slick

Attain coverage by   Then move down   Fish the
making short, successively   and repeat   entire drift.
longer casts...   the pattern...

~Typical Drift~

slic

Head~   Tailout~

slic

Sandbar   Eddy

~Steelhead Holding Positions~

Drift Boat Navigation

SAFETY FIRST:

WEAR A LIFE JACKET!!!

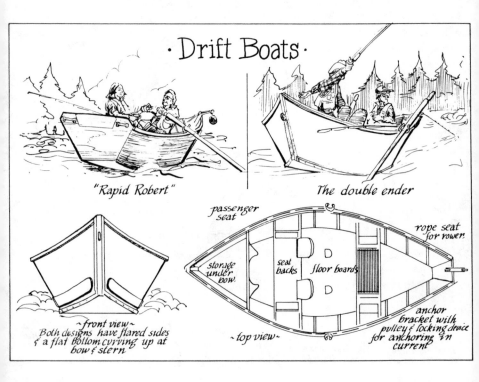

· Drift Boats ·

"Rapid Robert"

The double ender

~front view~
Both designs have flared sides
& a flat bottom curving up at
bow & stern

passenger seat

storage under bow.

seat backs

floor boards

~top view~

rope seat for rower.

anchor bracket with pulley & locking device for anchoring in current

MANUFACTURERS OF WHITE-WATER RIVER CRAFT

These companies can provide the river runner with boats. This list is not complete. Check whitewater periodicals and your local river sports stores for the names of other fine manufacturers.

ACHILLES INFLATABLE CRAFT (rafts)
P. O. Box 2287
Everett, Washington 98203 (206) 353-7000

ALUMAWELD BOATS, INC. (drift boats)
5681 Crater Lake Highway
Central Point, Oregon 97502 (503) 826-6161

AVON (drift boats)
West:
1851 McGaw Avenue
Irvine, California 92714 (714) 250-0880
East:
151 Mystic Avenue
Medford, Massachusetts 02155 (617) 391-5660

CLACKACRAFT (drift boats)
16969 S.E. 130th
Clackamas, Oregon 97015 (503) 655-9532

COLEMAN (canoes)
P. O. Box 1762
Wichita, Kansas 67201 (316) 261-3211

EASY RIDER (canoes, kayaks)
P. O. Box 88108
Tukwila Branch R-1
Seattle, Washington 98188 (206) 228-3633

EDDYLINE KAYAK WORKS (kayaks)
P. O. Box 281
Mukilteo, Washington 98275 (206) 743-9252

FISH RITE MARINE (drift boats)
5179 Crater Lake Highway
Central Point, Oregon 97502 (503) 776-0621

GREAT CANADIAN (canoes)
65 Water Street
Worcester, Massachusetts 01604 (617) 755-5237

HYDRA	(kayaks)
5061 S. National Drive	
Knoxville, Tennessee 37914	(615) 522-9902
LAVRO, INC.	(drift boats)
16311 - 177th Avenue, S.E.	
Monroe, Washington 98272	(206) 794-5525
MAD RIVER CANOES	(canoes)
P. O. Box 610E	
Waitsfield, Vermont 05673	(802) 496-3127
MARAVIA CORPORATION	(rafts)
P. O. Box 404	
Boise, Idaho 83701	(208) 322-4949
METZELER	(inflatables)
1044 Northern Blvd.	
Roslyn, New York 11576	(516) 484-4058
MOHAWK CANOES	(canoes)
P. O. Box 668	
Longwood, Florida 32750	(305) 834-3233
NIMBUS KAYAK SPECIALISTS	(kayaks)
2330 Tyner Street, No. 6	
Port Coquitlam, B. C., Canada V3C 2Z1	(604) 941-8138
NORTHWEST RIVER SUPPLIES	(rafts)
P. O. Box 9186	
Moscow, Idaho 83843	(208) 882-2383
PERCEPTION, INC.	(kayaks)
P. O. Box 686	
Liberty, South Carolina 29657	(803) 859-7518
PHOENIX PRODUCTS	(kayaks)
207 North Broadway	
Berea, Kentucky 40403	(800) 354-0190
RADON CRAFT	(drift boats)
Route 1, Box 550	
Bandon, Oregon 97411	(503) 347-3668
R B Boats	(drift boats)
40165 Mohawk River Road	
Marcola, Oregon 97454	(503) 933-2807

ROGUE INFLATABLES, INC. 8500 Galice Road Merlin, Oregon 97532	(rafts) (503) 476-3825
SEDA PRODUCTS P. O. Box 997 Chula Vista, California 92012	(kayaks) (619) 425-3222
SEVYLOR 6371 Randolph Street Los Angeles, California 90040	(inflatables) (213) 727-6013
SKOOKUM DORIES 1080 West Ewing Seattle, Washington 98119	(drift boats) (206) 282-8559
SUN RUNNER 3435 E. Anaheim Street Long Beach, California 90804	(inflatables) (213) 498-0887
UDISCO P. O. Box 15658 Salt Lake City, Utah 84115	(rafts) (801) 972-1330
WE.NO.NAH CANOE, INC. P. O. Box 2475 Winona, Minnesota 55987	(canoes) (507) 454-5430
WHITEWATER MANUFACTURING, INC. 1450 S.E. "M" Street Grants Pass, Oregon 97526	(rafts) (503) 476-1344
WILLIE'S R & D 1600 Skypark Drive Medford, Oregon 97504	(drift boats) (503) 779-4141

WEAR A LIFE JACKET!!!

NATIONAL CONSERVATION ORGANIZATIONS

These groups are dedicated in part or fully to the conservation of our nation's rivers.

American Canoe Association
P. O. Box 248
Lorton, Virginia 22079

American Rivers Conservation Council
322 Fourth Street, N.E.
Washington, D.C. 20002

American Whitewater Affiliation
P. O. Box 273
Powell Butte, Oregon 97753

Friends of the Earth
529 Commercial Street
San Francisco, California 94111

National Audubon Society
950 Third Avenue
New York, New York 10022

National Organization for River Sports
P. O. Box 6847
Colorado Springs, Colorado 80934

Sierra Club
530 Bush Street
San Francisco, California 94108

Wilderness Society
1901 Pennsylvania Avenue, N.W.
Washington, D.C. 20036